We at Birlinn are sorry, b additional biographical informatio Norman Maclean. All our requests for Norman's future aims and aspirations have been ignored. We can only plod down the well-worn path of his past achievements and triumphs. Two gold medals in 1967 (yawn), stand-up comedian to rival Billy Connolly (yawn) from the mid-seventies until well into the twenty-first century, the publication of his much acclaimed memoir, *The Leper's Bell*, in 2009, and the release of two 'entertainments' in 2011, *Dearest Dacha* and *Tricksters* just about covers it.

Reliable sources close to Maclean in Uist speculate that the author's reluctance to expatiate on works-in-progress derives from a recently acquired sense of modesty. Self-serving and self-promoting puff-pieces are anathema to this Salinger-like recluse. Fortunately, his take-off of ultra-individualists who go in for this kind of self-aggrandisement is well documented. 'Yeah, I'm just a kind of, like, generally creative person. I've written a dozen or so books for children in the past year, and I've also finished another two volumes of my autobiography. Oh, and yes, I'm submitting a thousand-page novel to the Booker committee next year . . .—blah, blah, blah.' No, the old guy, his friends insist, deplores self-promotion. He'd rather rub crumbly peat into his hair than be accused of blowing his own trumpet.

So, folks, with sincere apologies, that's the last of the Note on the A

Contracts

Norman Maclean

BIRLINN

First published as *Cùmhnantan* in 1996 by Clò Loch Abair
This edition published in 2011 by
Birlinn Limited
West Newington House
10 Newington Road
Edinburgh
EH9 1QS

www.birlinn.co.uk

ISBN 978 1 78027 065 4
eBook ISBN 978 0 85790 177 4

British Library Cataloguing-in-Publication Data
A catalogue record for this book is available from the British Library.

Designed and typeset by Iolaire Typesetting, Newtonmore
Printed and bound by Clays Ltd, St Ives plc

I dedicate this wee book to myself,
Norman Hector MacKinnon Maclean – a guy
who'll appreciate what a compliment a dedication is.

1

There was a bottle of Budweiser and a glass of Coke on the bar counter. Standing behind the counter, the short fat man who owned the place raised the bottle of beer and waved it towards the stage that was hard against the far wall about sixty feet to his left. The grey-haired man, crouched on a stool, made a half-turn to get a better view of it in the dark.

'I'll make this quick,' said the short man. 'Peavey 600 amp-head, Carlsbro combo amp – put your guitar through it, you want – and a Shure microphone.'

The grey-haired man swivelled on the stool so that the short man was directly opposite him. He drank a mouthful of Coke. 'Press the pause button, sonny,' he said. 'Is there a place where I can get into the kilt?'

'You can change in the kitchen,' the short man said. 'Go straight through that door up at the far end. Place's a mess, I'm afraid. Painters just left about an hour ago.'

'When are you thinking of starting?' the grey-haired man said.

The short man squinted at a Casio watch. 'Half past four now,' he said. 'The girls'll be coming in any time. You're here yourself around half past eight, so you can start . . . I don't know . . . round about nine.'

'Nine o'clock start,' the grey-haired man said. 'And when's the wrap?'

The short man consulted his watch again. 'Listen,' he said, 'you've only got to keep it going to midnight.'

The grey-haired man lit a cigarette, spun on the stool so that his back was to the short man and began bobbing his head, counting the chairs and tables from the far end where the stage was, all the way down to the function-room door. He stood up, and when he turned to face the short man, he smiled mockingly. 'This one I could do,' he said, 'in my sleep.'

'Just as long as you're conscious when you do it,' the short man said, glancing at his watch.

'Don't worry,' the grey-haired man said, 'I've been at this game for ages. Tomorrow you'll have a humph on your back taking all that money to the bank, and those that don't turn out'll be kicking themselves.'

'Uh-huh,' the short man said, 'but that's tomorrow. You've got to get through tonight first. It's tonight I'd be worried about, if I were you.'

'You're not, though,' the grey-haired man said. 'You don't have the talent to be me.'

'You sign the contract?' the short man said.

'I don't like contracts,' the grey-haired man said. 'A poxy little gig like this, we don't need them. A concert in a theatre, a good lift at the weigh-in, maybe I'd sign a contract. But a wee night in a place like this – how many does it hold? A hundred? Not worth it. Don't think I'll bother.'

'That's what I heard,' the short man said. 'I definitely heard that about you. "Campbell doesn't fancy contracts. Don Campbell doesn't work with a contract." Changed days now, Donald.' The short man pulled a sheet of paper out of his inside jacket pocket. 'Sign this.'

Donald Campbell took the contract between his thumb and forefinger. 'Whatever you say, sonny,' he said. 'You're the boss.' He stuffed the paper in his hip pocket.

'No, sign it,' the short man said. 'I really mean it, Donald. You want to do your thing on a handshake and that kind of bullshit, you do it. But working for me, in my hotel, you sign a contract. Okay?'

'Listen, Murdo,' Campbell said, 'you knew the trouble I got into the last time I signed a contract, you'd understand why I'm not a big fan of these things.'

'I heard something about that,' the short man said. 'Something about a trip to Venezuela, was it?'

'Don't ask,' Campbell said. 'I've promised to do the gig. I'll do it. Then, you give me the door money. End of story.'

'Beginning of story, son,' the hotel owner said. 'Contract makes a big difference. Today, when a contract exists between two people, you're protected. The other guy's protected, too. Say, you're looking for television work, and just about every moron among our sixty thousand bilingual population does want a taste of government money. And since it costs seventeen million pounds every year to service just over one per cent of Scotland's population, you'd be mad not to be thinking about that, Donald. The Beeb, say, approach you and they want to do a deal with you – they want you to write a comedy about a guy, a guy who . . . runs a ferry between two islands. They'll give you development money and ask you to write a script for them. You sign a contract. Both parties. You write the script, but they change their mind. They don't want to do the programme. You were obscene, or something – I don't know. You keep the money, though.'

Campbell took two paces towards the door and stopped. 'Murdo,' he said, 'I've known that for a long time.'

'Not finished yet,' the short man said. 'Maybe you went for the money at the beginning. Say you spent it – on drink or women, doesn't matter – and you didn't write the script. Then they can sue you, for your gold fillings. Take my word for it, the contract's important.'

'Contract's important,' Campbell said. He walked back to the counter. He dragged the contract out of his hip pocket, signed it and handed it to the short man.

'Welcome to the bright new world of Gaeldom,' the short man said. 'I started with a hotel on the west side of Lewis five years ago. Three years on I had a disco in Stornoway and three pubs out in the parishes. You know I'm telling the truth, Donald. You opened every one of them. Then, the year before last, I put my brother Kenneth into the Islander in Oban. You opened that one, too. Tonight, you'll open The Islander Two in Glasgow. Give them a night they'll enjoy, and next year you'll be opening The Islander Three in Edinburgh.'

'You want me to do the comic characters tonight?' Campbell said.

'No,' the hotel owner said. 'It'll be pretty rough in here tonight and I don't think the Govan punters are terribly keen on our sense of humour. If I was you, I'd keep with the singing all night.'

'Okay,' Campbell said, 'the songs all night it is.'

'Plenty of Gaelic songs,' the hotel owner said. 'There's a

4

mob of nurses and students from the Islands coming. Why didn't you bring that guy from Harris that plays the accordion? What do they call him? Calum Iain? He could have played for dancing, give you a break.'

'Not enough money for him,' Campbell said. 'Not enough money for me even.'

'I'm offering you a ton and a half,' the hotel owner said. 'Time was, you wouldn't have moaned about that.'

'Like you said,' Campbell said, 'changed days now.'

'So I noticed,' the hotel owner said. 'Smart suit you're wearing. Where did you get it? Venezuela?'

'Forget it,' Campbell said, 'and don't mention that place again.'

'You must have blown a packet over there,' the hotel owner said. 'Maybe I'll give you a small bonus at the end of the night.'

'How small?' Campbell said.

'Depends how good you do tonight,' the hotel owner said.

'Depends how good your memory is, too,' Campbell said. 'You not remember all the favours I've done for you in the past?'

'Yeah,' the hotel owner said, 'I'll give you another twenty pounds.'

'Twenty?' Campbell said. 'Are you from Tel Aviv or Tolsta? Way too low. What about my debts – I mean, how do I live on money like that? That won't keep me in drams, never mind wages.'

'It won't,' the hotel owner said, 'because you won't be getting any drams in here tonight. I've warned the staff. Anybody feeds you strong drink, they're sacked. I know you're off the stuff just now, but did you break out when you were in – when you were abroad?'

'You're not the only Teuchter with a hotel in Glasgow,' Campbell said.

'But I'm the only one with your signature on a contract,' the hotel owner said. 'Tonight, Donald. Nine till midnight. A hundred and seventy notes.'

'I've never gone for less than two hundred before,' Campbell said. 'And I'm not going for less this time either.'

'You're full of it, Donald,' the hotel owner said. 'Many's the time you've gone for a hundred and twenty from me back on the island, and before the night's out you're into me for a sub so you can go to a party with some little honey you'd make a father for. I've known you a long time.'

'Tell you what I'll do,' Campbell said. 'Because I'm in a bit of a tight spot just now, financially, I'll take a hundred and ninety.'

'Stuff it,' the hotel owner said. 'I only need to give you a hundred and fifty. I've offered a hundred and seventy.'

'What about a hundred and eighty, then?' Campbell said.

'Split the difference,' the hotel owner said. 'I'll make it a hundred and seventy-five.'

'Give me twenty-five just now, then,' Campbell said.

'No problem,' the short man said.

Campbell lifted the banknotes the hotel owner had laid on the counter, raised them to his lips and his expression changed: he smiled.

2

In Casa Angelo in the city centre the Italian waiter carrying a cappuccino and Calum Iain MacAskill came into Campbell's vision at the same time. MacAskill was from Rodel, and though his family owned fishing boats and earned a comfortable living, Calum Iain was interested only in accordion music. He took frequent trips to the mainland, often as far south as Glasgow and Edinburgh. He sat at the table next to Campbell. His hair was long and he wore oversized sunglasses. 'Hey, Donald,' he said. 'Your Peggy told me this is where you'd be, in the bosom of the *paisano*.'

'Take a look at yourself,' Campbell said. 'Do you work in a circus now or do you just like dressing like a clown?'

'We can't all afford to go to Ralphie Lauren for our gear,' MacAskill said. 'Where did you get the coat anyway? Venezuela?'

'Naw,' Campbell said. 'Wardrobe allowance I got from that independent mob – what are they called? Cu Chulainn, that it? Two buckled shots run it, and big Archie's daughter from Grimsay used to work for them as a runner.'

'Ossian Productions,' MacAskill said. 'And I heard these boys weren't so bent. Morag, big Archie's daughter, was telling me that the dark one, Crispin, made a move on her in the edit suite when they were cutting that programme you presented.'

'Isn't she the lucky one,' Campbell said.

'Do I detect a hint of envy?' MacAskill said.

'No,' Campbell said.

'Right,' MacAskill said. 'Couldn't be that Don Campbell, South Uist Comedy King, is missing a bit of bed fun these days, could it?'

'I've had my share of that,' Campbell said. 'Tell the truth, these women have finished me off. That's why I'm kind of doing the backstroke just now.'

'Not what Peggy says about you,' MacAskill said. 'Told me you never came home last night at all. Who's the new bird?'

'What?' Campbell said.

'Your new bird,' MacAskill said, smiling at the waiter as he arrived with a bottle of beer and a glass. 'Peggy's convinced you've got a bird. Says you've been out nearly every night since you came back from Mexico – Venezuela, I mean.'

'Holy Mother,' Campbell said. 'I'm just back from holiday, right? What's a guy supposed to do when he comes back from holiday? Am I supposed to sit like a lump by the fireside listening to my sister giving me grief all day? I've got to get out to meet people, mainly TV people. These meetings can last a long time.'

MacAskill started to pour the beer. 'Right,' he said. 'Peggy must be telling the truth, then.'

'You're really terrific at getting to know a guy,' Camp–

bell said. 'You'd like it if I told you everything that happened to me in Venezuela, wouldn't you? You bet you would. But I'm telling you nothing. Know this, Calum Iain? You'd make a great husband for our Peggy. Her the widow and you the inquisitor! The pair of you'd make a great couple. Spend the honeymoon wearing your mouths out talking about me. Figuring out how much money I spent while I was away.'

MacAskill raised his glass and drank a mouthful. 'Drink your coffee, Donald,' he said. 'No dough, I'll buy you another one.'

'Sunshine,' Campbell said, 'I'm so short that a cup of coffee doesn't hack it. What I'm looking for is a *croft* where they grow the coffee.'

'Hey,' MacAskill said, 'that's what sent you to Venezuela. Prospecting for a coffee plantation, were you? You were definitely looking for something.'

'I had plenty of money before I went to Venezuela,' Campbell said. 'That was then, this is now. What I'm looking for now is a big chunk of dough that'll pay my debts.' He drained the cappuccino and looked at MacAskill. 'Know anybody who's interested in a tenor saxophone?'

'A tenor saxophone,' MacAskill said.

'Yeah, a big metal thing with holes,' Campbell said. 'You stick it in your mouth and blow. And I've got a Washburn guitar I want to sell.'

'Between the Butt of Lewis and Barra Head,' MacAskill said, 'I don't know one person who plays tenor saxophone – except you. It's the accordion I play, mind. If you had a

Hohner Gola I could maybe get you two or three hundred for it. How big is this chunk of dough you need?'

'Two and half thousand,' Campbell said.

'I'd say,' MacAskill said, 'that's a pretty, well, *big* chunk. That why you didn't want me last night when you opened Wee Murdo's new place?'

'Och, that was only a wee daffodil tea party,' Campbell said. 'A favour for Wee Murdo, know what I mean? A couple of songs, a few gags and "welcome, goodnight and safe home". You know the kind of thing.'

'I certainly hear the music, but I can't make out the tune you're playing,' MacAskill said. 'Who was backing you?'

'Nobody,' Campbell said. 'Wasn't worth asking you. It's only a tiny place, and I took the guitar and the pipes along.'

'And now that it's job done,' MacAskill said, 'you want to punt the instruments? Some things never change, Donald, eh? You're forty-five now, can't get away with your usual line of bull with the young girls. "Just a bottle of wine and a curry, pet. I won't stay long. I'm strongly attracted to you, darling. Just let Donald take care of you." These days are gone, Donald. Time to sling all that foolishness.'

'Time for me to trap,' Campbell said. He took out his wallet.

'Listen, Donald,' MacAskill said, 'you ever thought about going back to doing live gigs? I'm up for it. I've had a ration of fishing. If you don't fancy getting back with Anna in Inverness, and you want to stay here in Glasgow, we could buy a flat. I've got the van. I'd do the driving. We'd let the good times roll again. How about it?'

'Calum Iain,' Campbell said, 'are you *nuts?* Like you say, I'm forty-five years of age. Like you say, it's time to sling the foolishness. And like you say, these days are gone. The main thing I'm after just now – like, today – is money.'

'There's money in the gigs,' MacAskill said.

'There's money in the fishing, too,' Campbell said, 'but that kind of work, both kinds, would kill a horse. You fancy leaving Lochgilphead at three in the morning, after taking your kidneys out trying to please a bunch of stoners, leaving the Argyll, early doors, with a drive to Ullapool in front of you so you can catch the Stornoway ferry at half past nine, with nothing at the other end but more alcoholics?'

'But the women were good, Donald, weren't they?' MacAskill said.

Campbell looked at the contents of his wallet and closed it rapidly. 'They were okay. When I quit the teaching in Inverness High School and went full-time into the business – maybe fifteen years ago – nobody was happier than me. I had a little house down on the Haugh, I had Anna, and the boys were happy in the primary school.

'Things were like that for about two years. Didn't touch a drop all that time. Worked day and night. Did that series for the BBC, *Who Else But Campbell?*, and everything was big money. Thing was, I was down in Glasgow and she was up in Inverness. Finally, I decided to take a trip to a sunnier place, but Anna wouldn't come along with me – she'd rather go to Lewis to her mother's and her sister's – so I had to go to Venezuela without her.'

11

'But you didn't go by yourself,' MacAskill said.

'I took this girl with me,' Campbell said. 'I don't know for sure, but I think I was trying to be a nice guy. I had the idea that was the kind of thing a big-timer in showbiz would do. You know: a nice little present for a kid who'd never seen much of the world before?'

'Donald,' MacAskill said, 'Rae MacAulay was only sixteen years old – if she was that – when you took off with her to Venezuela.'

'Sixteen going on forty,' Campbell said.

'Look, man,' MacAskill said, 'your own boys were nearly as old as her. Where did you hook up with her, anyway?'

'At the gigs,' Campbell said. 'She'd always show up at the concerts in Lewis or in Harris. Wanting an autograph or a CD or something. She was kind of cute and lively, and I invited her back to the hotel after the ceilidh. We'd a couple of glasses of brandy, she stayed, and before you could say "Bless you", Rachel's in my life.'

'And Anna's out of it?' MacAskill said.

'I wouldn't say that,' Campbell said, raising his head. 'Right enough, when me and the young lady in question came back from Venezuela, Anna didn't take long running me off the premises in Inverness, but it wasn't Rachel that really pissed her off. What really upset her was that I'd started drinking again. Should've heard her. "I don't give a damn, Donald, if you go with every whore on the island. I hope they're good to you. What I can't handle is you killing yourself with that horrible booze." I'd feel so guilty at how reasonable she was that I'd go for another blast and end up ten times worse.'

'Will she have you back?' MacAskill said.

'You'd have to ask her,' Campbell said. 'I think she would. If I knocked the drinking on the head, maybe she would. But, unfortunately, I haven't been able to do that – up till now, anyway. If I could get together a little money to fix up my grandfather's house in Uist, maybe we could go back home together. We'll see. I love her deeply. I don't think she hates me. When I go up to visit we don't fight, don't argue and we don't show one another up. Well, I try my best not to show her up.'

He stood up. He smiled at MacAskill. 'As the old folk used to say: "A man's got to be foolish for a time before he gets wise."'

'Why don't you take my advice, man?' MacAskill said. 'Start back on the gigs. That's what you know. You're good. I'm not stroking you, you're the best. Seems the people at the Islander had a terrific time last night. Wee Murdo would give you a residency like a shot, and we could go on safari at the weekends. A year or two's time you'd have enough money to do up the house in Uist, and you and Anna could get back together.'

'Well,' Campbell said, 'you're right in one way, boy. I can't look at the house in Uist unless I've got a good wad before I start. And there isn't a chance Anna'll come back to me if I don't have a place for us to stay. But you're wrong if you think anybody can make money traipsing round the Highlands and Islands like a tinker playing instruments, singing and trying to make people laugh. I've stopped all that foolishness. I've got my sights on something that's far, far bigger

13

than ceilidhs in pubs or concerts in halls out in the sticks.'

'What's that?' MacAskill said.

'Television,' Campbell said. 'Gaelic television. This STG crowd – *Sgioba Telebhisean Gàidhlig* – have got millions of pounds to spend on Gaelic programmes this year. And every year, little man. Index-linked. All I want are some crumbs when that cake's cut.'

'That's what I'm telling you, Donald.' MacAskill said. 'We should form a group – The Clansmen, or The Islanders – and try and get on the telly.'

Campbell placed his hand on the shoulder of MacAskill who was still seated at the table looking up at him. 'Listen to me, Calum Iain. You're as short-sighted as every other Gael. When you hear the word "television" you can't see further than the screen. You only have eyes for the pictures that people higher up have decided to broadcast. You're bewitched watching dots through clouded eyes. Oh, sure, you get a scabby little cheque and, if you're a good-looking dame, a nice wardrobe allowance to buy stylish gear so you'll look cool in front of the camera. But never in a thousand years will you make real money. The power lies behind the cameras. And the money. You ever think about those big noises up in Perth at North Television or over in Edinburgh at Albion TV, or even here at the Beeb – the dripping roast of a life they've got? In every company there's some fat old man slouched in a chair giving orders: "Hey, make this programme" and "Don't make that programme" and "Why don't you get Crispin as producer and Su as director?" That's the old guy I want to get close to. That's the old guy I want to *marry*.'

'How you going to manage that?' MacAskill said.

'I've already started,' Campbell said. 'You ever hear of Iomhaigh Productions? Some fellow from Back runs it? Used to be a lecturer at the uni? Got to know him and the Barraman who's along with him just before I left – before I took off for Venezuela.'

'I know Duncan, the lad from Barra,' MacAskill said. 'Well, I don't really know him but I know who he is. Didn't he used to work for the Beeb up in Stornoway? Wasn't he the guy who did *Greetings*?'

'The very one,' Campbell said. 'But he got smart, and left radio, or he got the elbow, I don't know. He left Stornoway, anyway, and he joined Maclean when the Prof formed Iomhaigh Productions. I get on pretty well with them. Well, I *used* to get on pretty well with them.'

'Did you have a fall-out?' MacAskill said.

'No,' Campbell said. 'Not yet. And we won't. That is, if I can raise two and a half thousand before the end of next week.'

MacAskill gazed at him intensely. He sighed. 'You get me worried when I hear you talking like that.'

'Forget it,' Campbell said. 'I'll get out of this by myself. I've been waiting all my life for an opportunity like this. There are people out there gambling. Millions of pounds on the table. I'd like a seat at that table. The only thing keeping me back is lack of funds. Two thousand, five hundred pounds. One way or another I'm going to get it.'

'Well,' MacAskill said, 'one thing's for sure. Nobody's

15

going to make two and a half thousand selling a saxophone and a guitar.'

'That's right, pal,' Campbell said. 'Remember that. Hold on to your accordion and don't sell it before the end of the month. Maybe you'll be needing it soon.'

3

At midnight in the Islander, when Campbell strolled in, the only customers left were three lads from Lewis pooling their money to buy a bottle of whisky before moving on to a party in someone's house. He sat on a stool in front of Gretta, a tall blonde from Skye, who was rinsing glasses.

'Is the man himself about?' Campbell said.

'Who's that?' the girl said.

'Hitler,' Campbell said. 'Skinny wee thing, very white face with scrubbing brush moustache, looks as if he should be working in a dwarf-throwing bar somewhere on Wall Street.'

The girl laughed and placed her elbows on the counter. 'Is Murdo expecting you?'

'Don't know,' Campbell said. 'Told me he'd give me some money. I did a ceilidh for him. Did that. Last night, if you remember, Gretta. And I've come for my money.'

'You were great, Donald,' the girl said. 'I almost died laughing when you told that one about the boy from Harris. Hold on a minute.' She walked up to the end of the counter, waved for him to follow, and approached a door bearing the legend *Manaidsear*. Manager. She knocked on the door and entered. She closed the door. Campbell remained standing outside.

The door opened once more. The blonde stuck her head out. 'He'll see you now.'

'Thanks, girl,' Campbell said, and he walked past her into the office.

'Donald,' Wee Murdo said, 'come on in, boy. Have a seat.'

Campbell sat on a settee in front of Murdo's desk.

'This is Gretta,' Wee Murdo said.

Gretta was almost six feet tall, ten stones, and she had heavy breasts.

'What part of Skye you from, Gretta?' Campbell said.

'She's from Uig,' Wee Murdo said.

'You know my mother, Donald,' Gretta said. 'Dolina. Dolina MacKinnon before she got married. She was from Sconser. Used to work in the hotels in Oban.'

'You don't say,' Campbell said.

Gretta smiled.

'What you doing round here this time of night?' Wee Murdo said.

'I was desperate to meet the daughter of an old girl-friend of mine. I thought, I don't know, if I took a little trip over to Govan late on a Saturday night I stood a good chance of getting mugged. On top of that, Murdo, I'm having my ears chewed off listening to my sister Peggy moaning about how I'm never home and I never give her enough money. Talking about that, think you've got a little dough to give me.'

'Gretta,' Wee Murdo said, 'away and get a Budweiser for me and a Coke for Donald.'

As soon as the blonde left the room, Campbell stood up

and perched on the edge of the desk so that he looked down on Murdo. 'Cosy wee set-up you've got here. I know quite a bit about pubs – drinking in them, getting drunk in them, killing myself working in them – but I haven't seen a first-line pad as good as this thing you and big Gretta have here. And you also had a first-class ceilidh here last night.'

'Wasn't a bad night at all,' Wee Murdo said.

'Murdo,' Campbell said, 'you had an exceptional night last night. Time to pay for it. Give me my money.'

'We'll talk about that later,' Wee Murdo said. 'Listen, Donald, where you living just now?'

'You know damn fine where I'm staying,' Campbell said. 'At Peggy's place. Me and my blessed sister, Johnny's widow, the sodium amytal, live in a hen coop in Partick. You know this, Murdo? My room's so small Anne Frank wouldn't have lived in it.'

'I've got a flat,' Wee Murdo said. 'Above the pub. Gretta's in it just now, but there's two bedrooms, and you're welcome to stay there.'

'Uh-huh,' Campbell said, 'and what would Gretta have to say about that?'

'She's totally hot,' Murdo said. 'Fancy her?'

Gretta came in carrying a tray. It held a bottle of Budweiser, a bottle of Coke and two glasses. 'Fancy who?' she said.

'You,' Campbell said. 'Murdo here's in a frenzy to get you and me upstairs together. Better believe it, darling: once upon a time, I'd have made a proper fool of myself over you. Come to think of it, that's what I did with your

19

mother. You're almost as pretty as her, too. See and tell her I was asking for her.'

'I don't know what you're on about,' Gretta said, shaking her head. She continued to stare at Campbell, however.

'Gretta, go outside,' Wee Murdo said.

'You know my boss here,' Gretta said, 'pure gentleman type.'

'I told you,' Wee Murdo said. 'Move yourself and get rid of those boys who're shouting out there.'

'To hell with you,' Gretta said. 'I heard what you said about me, I was out there – I heard you. "She's totally hot." You don't have the manners of a dog, Murdo. How'd you like it if I was to tell the girls how you amuse yourself in your spare time?'

The short man came out from behind the desk quickly and slapped her back-handed. 'Didn't I tell you to get out?' he said. 'That's what I want you to do. Get out!'

Campbell grabbed the hair of the short man and dragged him backwards until he collapsed on the settee. He threw a handkerchief towards the girl. He kept a firm grip on the hair of the short man until he was sure he had calmed down. 'Don't move, Murdo,' he said. 'She doesn't have to go anywhere either. Give me the money and I'll leave. Reckon you're not in the mood for conversation tonight, anyway.'

'Stay where you are, Donald,' Gretta said. 'Get as much money as you can off him, and when you're ready come up the stairs for a cup of tea or something. I'll be waiting for you.' She wiped her lips with the handkerchief and handed it back to Campbell. 'I'd like to hear more about what you and my mother got up to in Oban.'

Gretta stamped out on high heels and shut the office door with a bang.

'You ever go to bed with a woman . . .' Wee Murdo said, combing his hair.

'Sure,' Campbell said.

'You ever go to bed with a woman without a lot of fighting and aggravation?' Wee Murdo said. 'That's what I mean. I can see why some guys go to massage parlours. You go down there, you pick a looker, give her half a cenny and she does exactly what you tell her to do.'

'Time you stopped talking, Murdo,' Campbell said. 'Get the money and I'm out of here.'

'Hey,' Wee Murdo said, 'the money. What do I have to give you?'

'A cenny and a half,' Campbell said.

'I'll be with you in two ticks.' Wee Murdo got up and went out to the bar. After two minutes he returned. He had a white envelope in his hand. He handed it to Campbell. 'Count it,' he said.

'Don't need to,' Campbell said. He accepted the envelope and put it in his pocket. 'This is the last time I'll take money from you, Murdo. And I'll never work for you again either.' He turned to go.

'You've got to trap?' Wee Murdo said.

'I've got to get more money,' Campbell said. 'You better go after that girl and apologise to her.'

'As if,' Wee Murdo said. 'Listen, Donald, how'd you like three nights in here every week till the end of the year?'

'Wouldn't like it at all,' Campbell said. 'But I'd do it if the money was right.'

'I'd give you a hundred a night,' Wee Murdo said. 'If you fancied taking that Harris fellow along with you, that'd be okay. But you'd have to pay him. You'd have three hundred a week.'

'Three hundred a week,' Campbell said. 'That would come to fifteen grand for the entire year – right?'

'Something like that,' Wee Murdo said.

'Okay,' Campbell said.

'Okay?' Wee Murdo said. 'You really want to do it?'

'I didn't say I wanted to do it,' Campbell said. 'But I would do it on the condition that you write a cheque, tonight, made out to me for two and a half grand.'

'Hold on, Donald,' Wee Murdo said. 'I can't do that. That's . . . two and a half grand's too much. I mean, right away. Know what I mean: at the one time?'

'I know only too well, Murdo,' Campbell said. 'You're nothing but a bent little creep. An overweight little cockerel, likes to hit women – that's what you are. I need that two and a half thousand, but even if you gave it to me this very minute, I'd shove it up your backside.'

4

The offices of Iomhaigh Productions were situated in what used to be a ground-floor two-bedroomed flat in a tenement in Partick. On the right-hand side as one entered the hall there was a bathroom and kitchen. The two offices lay to the left. Seated at a desk in the smaller one, George Kerr was talking on the telephone. Since his elevation to the position of head of production at North Television more than a dozen years previously, it was an established daily practice of his to telephone at five-thirty Jean, his secretary at Studio North in Perth, any time he would be away on trips. He was wearing a grey flannel suit his wife had purchased for him in Austin Reed, and black Grenson brogues. Securing the collar of his white cotton shirt was a silk tie with abstract green and yellow stripes. All the time he was engaged with the telephone, his fingers of his right hand kept stroking the bracelet of the Rolex watch he had paid twenty dollars for to a Rastafarian from Jamaica he'd met on the beach at Fort Lauderdale the previous year when he and Liz had been on holiday.

He spoke: 'Look, Jean, tell Gordon this will take about another week.' He fell silent. 'Because, Jean, that's how long it's going to take me to get these playboys into shape.' He stopped speaking for ten seconds. 'Well, I suppose Sinclair's okay, or *will* be all right when I've finished with him, but Maclean's worse than useless.' He fell silent. 'He's an academic. Sure, he knows all the buzzwords. I hear stacks of chat about the "conventions of the genre" and the "paradigm of the programme". Uses "lead-in to the break" and "top of the programme" a lot, too. He talks a good programme, but the longer I've been down here the more I'm convinced Gordon made a serious error investing North's money in this Mickey Mouse operation. Investing in Maclean anyway.' He was silent once more. 'That's right,' he said. 'I'll be home the end of next week. Now, I've got Starsky and Hutch to see. Yes, I'm practising my Gaelic. *Latha math, ciamar a tha thu a' faireachdainn an-diugh*?' He hung up. He got up from the desk and walked out the office. When he heard the low voices coming out of the kitchen he stood in the hall for an instant before pushing open the kitchen door.

John Alex Maclean and Duncan Sinclair were standing with their backs to him and looking down at an open motoring magazine on the table. 'That's how I see you, Duncan,' Maclean said, placing his forefinger on a glossy picture of a Mitsubishi Shogun. 'Just imagine, man, what a babe-magnet you'd be if you drove something like that.'

Kerr coughed politely. '*Iain*,' he intoned, '*ciamar a tha thu a' faireachdainn an-diugh*? Duncan, *ciamar a tha thu a' faireachdainn an-diugh*?'

'Feeling good, George,' Sinclair said. 'Who wants coffee?'

'Me,' Maclean said. 'I definitely need something to revive me. I'm completely burned out.'

24

'I do not want coffee, Duncan,' Kerr said. 'Thank you. And if you could hold off for a minute or two, John Alex, I'd be grateful if you'd spare the time for a brief meeting next door. You too, Duncan. I'll probably need some stuff printed off from the database.' He pulled the door open and inclined his head. 'After you, gentlemen.'

The three of them entered the big office. Sinclair sat down behind a desk on which there stood a MacBook Pro laptop. Kerr took a seat from where he could comfortably view the computer screen. Maclean remained standing in the middle of the floor. 'Don't take too long, George,' he said. 'I'm so tired I'm fit to drop.'

Kerr raised his head. 'You do look a bit rough.'

'No wonder,' Maclean said. 'Turned in at the Stag Inn in Stornoway – oh, about three in the morning, something like that. Up again at five. Down to Tarbert, then across to Uig. Dinner in Inverness along with a girl I met on the ferry. Then a murderous mad dash down the road. I'm absolutely knackered.'

'What were you doing in Stornoway?' Kerr said.

'I had a meeting with Flora,' Maclean said. 'In the headquarters of the STG. Yesterday. At three o'clock.'

'Wait a minute,' Kerr said. 'You went to Stornoway – on what, Monday? To talk to Flora Macdonald of the *Sgioba Telebhisean Gàidhlig*. About our programme *Take a Chance* – I mean, *Cuid do Chroinn* – I hope?'

'I had an extensive agenda,' Maclean said. 'I don't know that I have the leisure to review for you every topic we discussed, but rest assured, George, an update on the current status of *Cuid do Chroinn* was included.'

'What is this "extensive agenda" and "update" stuff?' Kerr said. He turned to Sinclair. 'Mr Sinclair, since you appear to be the sole officer of Iomhaigh Productions not unaware of the new technology, and since you both share a mutual frame of reference provided by the Gaelic language and a common educational background – Glasgow University, wasn't it? – please inform your partner that for the purposes of long-distance communication, people who may not have the leisure to make reviews avail themselves of a couple of things just out. They're called the mobile phone and email.'

'George, George,' Maclean said, 'I don't find your laboured attempts at humour very funny. But of course you don't have a degree, do you? I won't bore you with the inventory of reasons that persuaded me that my presence in Stornoway yesterday was justified. Even a big-time executive producer like yourself will appreciate that it would be extremely difficult to monitor an audition by email.'

'What does this "audition" crap mean?' Kerr said. 'What do you know about auditioning anyone? Is this in connection with our – with *Cuid do Chroinn* or with Iomhaigh?'

Sinclair raised his head and stared at Maclean. 'I didn't know about this, John Alex. I didn't know you went to Stornoway to *audition* someone.'

'Well,' Maclean said, 'I don't tell you everything I'm going to do when I go off on company business.'

'Oh, bullshit, Maclean!' Kerr said. 'I know fine what you get up to when you go off on one of your trips. What did she – this is a chick you're auditioning, right? – what'd she do for you, eh? Find a new way to do it in the bath? Recite *The Eternal Surge of the Sea* while feeding you whisky through a baby's bottle? What could she possibly do for you that any of your little groupies in the Ben Lomond couldn't?'

'Celibacy has never struck me as a desirable aspiration for a divorced man,' Maclean said. 'Fortunately, in the particular area of enterprise in which I now find myself, the brave new world of Gaelic television production, nubile and eligible ladies abound. Lecturing at the university provided the odd opportunity, admittedly, although I must confess I probably had a less agreeable social life than I enjoy today. Help! I've got to call – I've got a phone call to make.'

'Who's the lucky woman?' Kerr said.

Maclean looked around carefully as if making sure no others were in the room overhearing him. He lowered his voice. 'Flora Macdonald, or, as she's known in Benbecula, *Flòraidh Dhòmhnaill Anndra*, vice-chair of the STG and a good friend of Iomhaigh Productions.'

'She phoned about an hour ago,' Sinclair said. 'She was delighted with the projections you gave her for *Cuid do Chroinn*. She asked me to thank you for them. What a cheek she had! It was me who put them together, and you're the one who gets the credit. Did you tell her it was me who slaved over all these figures for that series?'

Before Maclean could answer, Kerr had another question for him. 'What are the committee saying?'

'What about?'

'About . . . concerning our series. What are they saying about *Take a Chance* – ah, *Cuid do Chroinn?*'

'They adore the programme idea,' Maclean said. 'Though I myself think it's nothing but cheap froth that bombed in English and will be measurably worse in Gaelic, they liked the other ideas I put to them.'

'What did they think of my idea?' Sinclair said. 'Did you tell them about my story?'

'Never mind about that just now, Duncan,' Maclean said. 'We'll go out for a pint shortly. Just relax for a moment and you can show Mr Kerr how slick you were in preparing *Cuid do Chroinn.*' He passed a cheque over to George Kerr. 'There you go, George. With kindest regards from the STG, a cheque for twelve thousand pounds, part of your fee for being the nominated broadcaster, or perhaps I should say, North Television's "production fee". You take that one, and the next cheque that comes in, Iomhaigh will take that one. Though I don't like to tempt providence, I'm pretty sure we'll all be drowning in money from the *Sgioba Telebhisean Gàidhlig* in the future.' He smiled. 'Aren't we the lucky boys!'

The printer on the desk started to clatter and pages began to pour out of the device. Kerr grabbed them one by one as they came out, and he carefully read each sheet. 'This is good, Duncan,' he said to Sinclair. 'This is really quite good.'

'Well,' Sinclair said, 'the casting of the presenter, the team captains and the "celebs" was all done by John Alex. He did the selection of directors and crew and stuff as well. I handled the correspondence and most of the budget.'

28

'What's this? TX12?'

'Oh, that's just BBC shorthand for transmission date of programme. The series goes out early next year.'

Kerr stuffed the papers into his briefcase and looked straight at Sinclair. 'You worked for the Beeb, didn't you?'

'Three and a half years,' Sinclair said. 'I was only a radio producer over in Edinburgh, but they sent me on a course – that is, I *attended* a course for television directors down in London for three months. They themselves consider that they offer the best training in the world. I don't know. All I know is that I suffered brutal treatment at their hands when they got rid of me. "The Corporation, young man will not tolerate drunks. We have decided to attempt it without you. You're going to love the freedom of the independent sector. We hear the financial climate in Gaelic broadcasting is about to improve dramatically. Think of what you'll save in pension schemes and mortgage repayments when you're without a regular job or a home." Bastards.'

'That's where you're wrong,' Kerr said. 'The television companies don't owe you anything. Television companies are not charitable institutions. We are commercial enterprises. If you had been working for North, Duncan, instead of the BBC, when you had your little run-in with the law, we might have arranged counselling on alcohol abuse for you. On the other hand, we might have cut our losses and let you go, just as the Beeb did.'

'You ever work for them?' Sinclair enquired.

'We know he didn't,' Maclean said. 'That's why he didn't get the post of CEO at North the year before last when he applied for it. The man who got it, he'd been working in England with one or two big companies down there. And at the beginning of his career, it was at the BBC News Department here in Glasgow that Gordon Anderson learned his trade.'

'Who told you,' Kerr said, 'that I applied for the post of CEO?'

'Everybody in the whole wide world knows that,' Maclean said. 'And everybody knows that you made a run to become MD of Albion TV. They wouldn't look at you, George. "We limit the selection of candidates for the post of MD to those who have had significant experience at an executive level with either the BBC or one of the larger companies in the independent sector." That's what I heard anyway.'

'Who told you that?' Kerr said.

'I think,' Sinclair said, as he placed elastic bands round bundles of cheques and passed them over to Kerr, 'that these are all correct. I can't stay here any longer listening to the pair of you bickering.' He got to his feet and took a couple of steps towards the door. 'Whistle if either of you needs me.'

'You're going nowhere, Duncan,' Maclean said. 'And you're not going anywhere either, George. You stayed too long with the one company – how long have you been at North? Thirty years? You're a dinosaur, George. For you, executive producer – or, more accurately, broadcaster's bagman – to a callow independent Gaelic television company engaged in the production of an inane game show funded by the STG is about as good as it's going to get.'

'I don't know if it's going to be good,' Kerr said, extracting two cheques from a bundle and placing them to one side. 'But I feel it's going to be quite challenging. What do you know about these cheques from the *Cuid do Chroinn* chequebook?'

'You attribute to me powers I don't possess,' Maclean said. 'Though I do possess a PhD, something an under-achiever like yourself can't appreciate, I don't have the second sight. Since I don't understand what you're on about, I'd have to look at the cheques that seem to be worrying you unduly. I won't do that. I have no interest in them.

'When I approached Gordon early in the year with a written proposal for *Cuid do Chroinn*, I made sure he was fully cognisant with all that. When I went to Stornoway first of all to talk to the business manager of the Council, it was solely about the programme format I spoke. I was not concerned with cheques. When I realised I'd have to hire someone who'd look after the financial side of things, I invited the man from Barra who's sitting next to you to come in with me. He loves cheques. You, it appears, like them, too. Why *is* that?' He walked over to the desk and pointed a finger at each of them in turn. 'Because you don't have half an ounce of imagination between the pair of you.'

'Now, John Alex,' Sinclair began.

'Don't give me any of that "Now, John Alex" stuff,' Maclean said. 'Did you notice the nameplate on the outside door?'

'No,' Kerr said.

31

'That's what I thought,' Maclean said. 'What it says is Iomhaigh Productions Ltd – Dr J.A. Maclean. I'm the man who founded this company. I'm the man who established a friendly relationship with Anderson at North Television and with Flora Macdonald at the STG. I'm the one who obtained funding from them in order to make *Cuid do Chroinn*. That's the reason you're all in work just now. And that's the reason I'm off to make a cup of coffee for myself this very minute.'

He turned on his heel and marched out of the office.

Kerr lifted both cheques, placed one in front of Sinclair and kept the other one in his right hand. 'What's this, Duncan?' he said.

'Five hundred and forty-nine,' Sinclair said, 'made out to Mario Funaro Ltd on the third of February? I'm afraid I don't – wait a minute, I remember now. That's the Armani suit John Alex bought in the Italian Centre before he appeared in that programme about the Gaelic Television Resource. It's being broadcast sometime in the summer down here in the Lowlands. I don't think you guys are showing it until autumn.'

'Excuse me,' Kerr said. 'Do I understand you properly? Are you telling me that you knew all the time that the Prof was spending company money on himself? Money that was ring-fenced for a particular programme?'

'I know,' said Sinclair, 'that he owns Iomhaigh Productions, and I know that he who hath, shall receive more.'

'Uh-huh,' Kerr said. 'That's what he says. But did you ever consider that he might not be telling the truth?'

'No,' said Sinclair. 'I don't care. 'I'm just grateful that

John Alex gave me a job. And I can do this job. I can put together a television programme as well as anyone can. I like the work. Certainly, there are times when I don't like how profligate John Alex can be with the chequebook, but just as long as he leaves a scabby coin or two to pay my salary at the end of the month, I'm pretty much half satisfied.'

'Half satisfied?' Kerr said.

Sinclair looked towards the door. 'Well, I'll put it like this. I don't think John Alex distinguishes a clear line between personal and business expenses.'

'Please be so good,' Kerr said, 'as to amplify that observation.'

'I remember that cheque,' Sinclair said. 'The Prof breezed in here shortly after New Year wearing a sharp Italian suit and I said, "Was Father Christmas good to you?" Because you've got to remember that until then John Alex looked as though he got his clothes off the rails of Oxfam shops.

'And he says: "Like the suit, Duncan?" And I say: "Yeah." And he says: "Yeah? That all you have to say about an Armani suit I got in my very good friend Mario's boutique? Do you know how much I paid for this beautiful suit?" And I say: "No, what did you pay for it?" Because I knew it was kind of like my money he used to pay the Italian. I work for Iomhaigh Productions. Iomhaigh is kept alive by the Gaelic Television Resource. I reckon I had every right to ask him how much he'd paid out of my stash. "Right," he says. "I signed a cheque from the Iomhaigh Productions *Cuid do Chroinn* chequebook. A

33

real bargain, I only paid just short of six hundred for the suit." And what did I come back with? "Oh, John Alex, that's all right. The sheriff was so sweet when he sentenced me to two hundred hours Community Service. He told me if he ever saw me again in his court – well, he had another little stroke to play. I wouldn't have to bother going out with the other bad boys to dig gardens and paint walls – it'd be prison for me." And I wasn't really joking when I told him this. But, as usual, anything the Prof doesn't like, he doesn't hear.'

Kerr smiled at Sinclair. 'You're almost as thick as he is. And that's something. If he didn't have all those bimbos round about him he wouldn't be able to put on his pyjamas at bedtime.'

'Listen,' Sinclair said. 'These chequebooks are none of my business. John Alex has them all. He doesn't ask for my advice before he puts his name to a cheque.'

'So it seems,' Kerr said as he pushed the other cheque in Sinclair's direction. 'Perhaps we can lose the one to the Italian, but it won't be easy to hide this other one. What is West End Travel?'

'They're the people,' Sinclair said, 'who purchase train tickets for us.'

'That's some journey you guys went on,' Kerr said. 'How?'

'You could,' Kerr said, 'have gone round the world by rail at this price. Twice.'

'What,' Sinclair said, 'do the figures say?'

'The figures,' Kerr replied, 'say: two thousand, four hundred and ninety-five pounds.'

34

Sinclair clapped his right hand over his mouth. He closed his eyes for two seconds. 'Well, the man who can answer any questions you may have has just returned.'

Maclean entered carrying a cup of coffee. 'We need to have a girl for in here,' he said. 'She could make coffee for us, answer the phone, type up the scripts for us – stuff like that. It would raise the tone of the office if we had a well put-together young girl as a buffer between me and the supplicants.'

'John Alex,' Kerr said, 'why did you write a cheque for two and a half grand to West End Travel?'

'That was *Airgead-leasachaidh*,' Maclean said. 'Development money I invested in a writer.'

'For *Cuid do Chroinn*?' Kerr said.

'Certainly,' Maclean said.

'Who,' Kerr asked, 'was the beneficiary of this munificence?'

'Donald Campbell,' Maclean replied.

'Donald Campbell?' Kerr said. 'Who is Donald Campbell?'

'He's the presenter,' Maclean said, 'of *Cuid do Chroinn*.'

'What,' Kerr said, 'is he going to develop for us? Holiday snaps from the Caribbean?'

'As a matter of fact,' Maclean said, 'that's where he was headed. To do some writing.'

'What writing does he have to do?' Kerr said. 'It's a game show. He just has to ad lib. He can do that, can't he?'

'If you acquainted yourself to a greater degree with our culture,' Maclean said, 'you'd know that Don Campbell has had a distinguished career in stand-up comedy.'

'That's right,' Kerr said. 'He's also had a distinguished career as a drunk and philanderer, the way I hear it. Of course, in your culture the latter is considered a distinction rather than a liability.'

'Listen,' Maclean said. 'In my not so humble opinion, Campbell could do *Cuid do Chroinn* from a telephone kiosk. You want to tell me about talent in the bilingual community? What's your next project for today? Are you going to deliver three sacks of peat to Lochboisdale?'

'No,' Kerr said. 'I'm going to find out why you gave two and a half thousand pounds to Campbell – in addition to the fee you offered him for presenting *Cuid do Chroinn*.'

'Och,' Maclean said, 'there's not much money for him in *Cuid do Chroinn*. He knocks off twelve programmes in four days – two, four, four and two on the last day of shooting – and we give him, I'm not too sure, something like two hundred notes for each programme. That's not a fortune. And perhaps something better will emerge out of the development money.'

'I don't care,' Kerr said, 'if *Jurassic Park 2* emerges from the two and a half grand. Campbell will have to pay back that money. Iomhaigh Productions had no mandate to disburse one brown penny of development money. That is beyond your remit. You should be striving to produce a good programme. And the name of that programme is *Cuid do Chroinn*.'

'*Cuid do Chroinn*,' Maclean said. 'I'm not going to stop at *Cuid do Chroinn*. I am focused on the future. I, sorry, we – me and Duncan here – are chock-full of ideas for Gaelic television programmes. And we'll make them, too.

Gordon, he's one of your lot, and the Big Man at Albion and the members of the STG are all on my side. There's so much money in the Gaelic Television Resource that it'll last for ever – the annual seventeen million cost of BBC Alba's dedicated Gaelic channel is almost thirty per cent of BBC Scotland's programme budget – and this financial aid is targeted at us, the ones who're fluent in Gaelic. It won't be long now, George, until we won't need the likes of you with your feeble Gaelic and your paranoid scrutiny of every pound of expenditure.'

'Well,' Kerr said, 'I could argue with you about Iomhaigh's grand plans for Gaelic programming or whether you personally will have any part in them. And I certainly don't share your views about the bottomless nature of the Gaelic Television Resource. Moreover, if you fondly imagine that established broadcasters who have been in the business for longer than two minutes are quietly going to turn their backs on this new and welcome source of income and leave the field clear for the Gaels, then I suggest you scuttle back to the academic life and resume your career in sociology or bra-pinging, or whatever kept you out of the road of the buses.'

'Wait a minute,' Maclean said.

'I'll wait,' Kerr said, 'until you start shooting *Cuid do Chroinn* in our studio in Perth. When's that? Six weeks' time. I'll be with you for a while yet. And you're right – my Gaelic is less than fluent – so I'll say this very slowly. While I'm executive producer of this series, I'll be scrutinising every item in your budget intensely. We're talking one of your historian colleagues at the university

37

examining the Rosetta Stone here. Our little epic, gentlemen, has been funded by the Gaelic Television Resource under the administration of the *Sgioba Telebhisean Gàidhlig*, and our sole remit is to produce a funny game show. No money will be spent on suits created by homosexuals whose surnames end in vowels. Nor will we subsidise trips to the sun for broken-down whisky tenors. One other thing, Duncan.'

'What's that?' Sinclair said.

'Give me,' Kerr said, 'Campbell's address. And his phone number. I'd like a wee word with him.'

5

Donald Campbell came out of Queen Street Station at half-past one, on the dot. He walked quickly westward until he came to Buchanan Street where there stood a bank of telephone booths.

Inside one of the booths, Campbell inserted a coin into the slot and dialled his sister's number. 'Peggy? Donald here. Look, my mobile's gone flat so I'll be quick.' He listened for a couple of seconds. 'You're terribly funny, Peggy. Must be genetic coding. I'll do the jokes here.' He stopped talking. 'I went up to Inverness to see the kids . . . and Anne. Aye, in Dalneigh.' He paused. 'Fine, everybody's fine.' His mouth turned down in disapproval. 'What do you mean, did she give me money?' He pressed the receiver to his ear. 'I wouldn't ask her for a sun-tanned coin.' He pursed his lips. 'Dave gave me a sub, if you must know. He and I were pretty pally at one time when we formed Ness Recordings.' He remained silent for three seconds. 'Two hundred pounds.' He listened intently. 'I've got three hundred and fifty in my pocket right now, Peggy, and I've another two thousand to get.' He spoke irritably. 'That's what I've been trying to tell you. I lost that much in Venezuela and I'll have to give it back before I start on this damn programme *Cuid do Chroinn*.' He listened again. 'I don't know, Peggy – unless you help me out.' He held the

39

squawking receiver away from his ear for a full five seconds before resuming his conversation. 'Look, Peggy, I was only kidding. I'll get it, no problem.' He listened to his sister for quite a long while. 'Aye, aye, Peggy, very soon.' He allowed a spark of anger into his voice. 'Look here, woman, I know that. I'm telling you you'll get your money just as soon as I get mine.' He fell silent once more. 'Now, remember, Peggy – anybody phones looking for me, tell them I won't be home for a day or two, okay?' There was a brief pause. 'I'll spend a couple of nights with a friend of mine over in Govan.' Campbell's grip tightened on the receiver as he listened. 'When was this?' He stepped on the answer. 'Right. His name was Kerr, eh?' His words came in a rush. 'Listen, if he phones again, tell him I've just signed for Celtic as an attacker and I'm away to Milan to play for them in the European Cup.'

Campbell replaced the receiver on the cradle. He arranged a fistful of small change on the shelf in front of him and, after consulting a little address book, began to punch buttons once more. He spoke. 'Is John Alex in?' After a short delay he started to speak. 'No, no, you can't have my phone number. I'm in a public phonebox. Is this Duncan? Put John Alex on immediately, Duncan. Tell him it's Campbell.' There was another pause. 'John Alex? I'm glad I got you in. Listen, it seems the wee black pudding has been looking for me.' Pause. 'Yeah, wee Kerr.' There was another delay. 'I know that. Our Peggy told me he phoned yesterday. This is what you'll tell him: Campbell will be back at the beginning of the week – tell him I went up to Inverness to speak to my accountant – and that I'll make good the development money.' He fell silent once more. 'No, didn't write one word. What it is . . . I'll have to find the money first of all, and then I've got to give it back.' Another beat. 'Remember to tell him I'm pawing the turf waiting to get started on *Cuid do Chroinn*.' Yet another beat. 'I'll talk to him this Monday coming. At the Iomhaigh offices.' He remained silent again, and gave a heavy sigh. 'John Alex, I didn't say I'd have the money on Monday. I said I'll meet him on Monday, and I suppose by that time I'll have a better idea of when I'll be able to pay you back.' He listened for a short while. 'I know it's not your fault. Cheers, mate.'

He replaced the receiver, gathered up his change and ducked out from under the canopy. As soon as he emerged he saw a youth of about twenty or so standing much too close to him and scowling ferociously. 'Hope she's good-looking, pops,' he said. 'All I can say, I hope she's a looker, you take as long as that on the phone. Got yoursel' a promise for the night, eh?'

'Oh, she's good-looking all right,' Campbell said. 'Too tall for a wee smout like you, though. You ever go over to sunny Govan to tackle this lassie, you'd have to grab an ice-pick and yodel.'

'That'll be right, Jimmy,' the youth said, his eyes widening as though he vaguely recognised Campbell. 'Wait a minute, Ah know who you urr. Ah'm sure. So Ah'm urr. You're yon Teuchter guy oan the telly. Ye cannae say ye urrnae. Yon comedian guy, urrn't ye? Does the Gaelic 'n 'at, right? Goany say somethin' funny. In English.'

'Sure,' Campbell said. 'Eff off, Agnes.'

6

At eleven o'clock on Saturday morning in the outer
office of Gus Miller, head of production at Albion Television, on the third floor of a handsome building half-
way down Leith Walk in Edinburgh, Donald Campbell
suffered a severe nicotine fit. He got up from the leather
couch, opened a packet of Winston as he constantly
scanned the three television monitors on the wall in front
of him.

The woman spoke politely. 'I'm sorry, Mr Campbell,'
she said. 'If you're really desperate for a smoke, you could
go to the men's room just across the corridor. I'll give you
a knock when Gus's ready for you.'

Campbell said that was fine, and he entered the large
tiled room with four stalls, their doors wide open. In a
corner of the room above a giant mirror there were two
more television sets on a steel shelf. Campbell glanced
away from the cartoon that was being shown, and, after
lighting up a cigarette, looked at his reflection in the
mirror.

He wore a blue Hugo Boss suit with a white Swiss
cotton shirt. He was tieless. His feet were encased in two-
toned, black and white, Moreschi loafers. On his wrist he
sported a Longines stainless-steel watch with a black
leather strap. He ran a comb through his thick grey hair,

buttoned up his jacket and, almost immediately, unbuttoned it again.

He sat himself down in a plastic chair in front of the television receiver. For the following ten minutes he lost himself in the antics of the cat and the mouse. The soggy remains of two cigarettes were turning brown in the wash-hand basin when he heard the knock on the door.

Campbell spoke: 'Yes?'

The female voice said: 'Mr Miller will see you now, Mr Campbell.'

Campbell buttoned his jacket and followed the woman into Miller's office. The two men shook hands. The head of production at Albion Television was dressed in a teal-coloured linen jacket by Valentino, a lemon shirt and chinos by Ralph Lauren, and Timberland slip-ons. One would think, looking at Miller's forty-year-old face, that he was either allowing his beard to grow or he was just learning to shave with a razor. 'Welcome to our patch, Donald,' he said. 'My, you've fairly got the sun. You're looking really well, man.'

'I'm just a week back from Venezuela.'

'How did that grab you?'

'Pretty strongly,' Campbell said. 'I was researching material about a man from Perthshire – Griogair Mac-Gregor was his name – who gave Simon Bolivar tremendous assistance in the struggle for independence from Spain in the nineteenth century.'

'Right, Donald,' Miller said. 'And I've got an appointment with Angelina Jolie in Haymarket tonight. Were you chasing women and epic highs as usual?'

'Perhaps I wasn't entirely drug-free all the time, but there's no doubt in my mind that the women over there are stunningly beautiful and well worth chasing after.'

'Uh-huh,' Miller said, 'I've heard that. But never mind all that just now. Do you think you'll get material for a programme out of your research?'

'Griogair's life-story,' Campbell said, 'would make a great documentary. Maybe even a drama.'

'Why don't you write a proposal for the STG? Round about five thousand words – that should do it. If you've already done all the research, you'd only need a day or two to write it up. What do you think?'

'Well,' Campbell said, 'I'd really like to do something like that. But when did you say . . . when would you be looking for the proposal?'

'Monday,' Miller said. 'Monday, first thing in the morning. I'll have a look at it and if I think it'd be suitable for the STG – that is, if any programme that'd come out of it wouldn't be too dull, or too like something the Beeb might do – I'll give you . . . oh, a thousand pounds.'

'A thousand pounds,' Campbell said. 'I'd say that was, that's, a thousand pounds would be wonderful.' He stopped talking and drew a deep breath. 'That is satisfactory. When would I get the money, Gus?'

'Right now,' Miller said, 'if you want. Well, half up front today and another five hundred on Monday morning.' He lifted the phone and spoke softly into the mouthpiece. 'Elaine, would you prepare a standard first-look contract in favour of a Mr Donald Campbell, please?' He listened. 'For research on, oh, put down, "for research on Venezuelan project".' He listened once again. 'Oh, that's right. I forgot. Accounts are closed today.' He listened again. 'No, that's okay, Elaine. I'll make out a personal cheque to Mr Campbell.' He stopped speaking and looked over towards Campbell. 'That's alright, isn't it?' He raised a finger and smiled when Campbell nodded his head in agreement that he was happy with that. He directed his voice to the mouthpiece once more. 'In five minutes or so, Elaine. Thank you.'

Miller put down the receiver and turned towards Campbell, a wide grin on his face. 'She'll be in with a cheque shortly. Now, Donald, although I'm always delighted to come to an agreement with the likes of yourself, a writing project wasn't exactly what I had in mind when I received your phone call yesterday.' He paused for a beat. 'Do you know Carol Macleod, the head of our Gaelic department?'

'Yes,' Campbell said.

'Well, she's over in Islay this week filming a programme about the distilleries there. It'll go out in the spring of next year sometime. I'm expecting her – she's due back tonight, and she'll be in the office all day on Monday. I was just wondering if it might be a good idea for the three of us to have a bite of lunch together on Monday.'

'Were you?'

'Yes,' Miller said. 'She was telling me on the phone last night – I mean I know this – that she was in a spot of difficulty with a proposed series of light entertainment programmes that we're obliged to fund out of our own

46

resources without financial assistance from the Gaelic Television Resource.'

'What do you mean by a "spot of difficulty"?' Campbell said.

'She'll tell you herself,' Miller said, 'when we go for lunch on Monday. I'm pretty sure you'll be extremely well paid if you do as she asks. You could do with a bit of money, couldn't you, Donald?'

'You tell me where the old guy who's giving out the money lives, and my heels will be clipping my backside as I sprint for his house.'

The shadow of a smile flitted over Miller's face. 'Are you still doing the ceilidhs, Donald?'

'Odd nights,' Campbell said. 'Why?'

Miller pretended not to have heard him. 'And how's your ongoing battle with the booze going?'

'We've an armistice just now,' Campbell said.

'Glad to hear it,' Miller said. 'Because, if you promise to do this work for Carol, and you go on the piss, I'll come after you. You better believe it. Even though you might be safely tucked away in South Uist or in London, I'll find you. And what are you going to do if you're taking a stroll round about Eochar and you see a couple of burly strangers coming towards you with sticks in their hands? You're going to say a wee prayer, that's what you're going to do, because anybody who harms me or mine – anybody who lets me down, I mean – will pay dearly.'

Campbell lifted his head. 'Whoa, Gus,' he said, 'you don't have to show your macho-man credentials just yet. There's been no agreement on any work Carol may have for me. When I come to an agreement with her on Monday – if we do agree then – you can start your threatening sermons then.'

'Oh, I know you'll come to an agreement,' Miller said. 'There's big money attached to this. And you like money, don't you, Donald? There's enough money in this project to keep your accountant happy for a long time. I came on heavy with you because I didn't want either of you – you or Carol – to be embarrassed on Monday. Know what I mean?'

'Sure,' Campbell said. 'Oh, you've just reminded me – I can't meet with you on Monday.'

'Why not?'

'Because,' Campbell said, taking out his Winston packet, 'because – listen, I'm telling you the truth – I've got a meeting in Glasgow on Monday. With my accountant.'

'At what time?'

'In the morning,' Campbell said.

'You listen,' Miller said. 'I'm telling *you* the truth. You've got a choice here, Donald. Go to the meeting in Glasgow and hear bad news, probably. Come through here on Monday morning with a slender file and you'll get five hundred pounds cash, a good meal and perhaps a contract worth many times more than that from Carol. Why don't you phone him and say you'll meet him in the afternoon?' He pushed the telephone over to Campbell.

'You're right,' Campbell said. 'I'll reschedule the meeting with the accountant for another day. 'He suffered a brief coughing fit. 'I'll phone him this afternoon. He should be at home then.'

'We'll see you Monday morning, then?'

'Definitely,' Campbell said. 'About half past nine?'

'Nine. Don't I have to look at the MacGregor story before the three of us go out?'

'You do,' Campbell said. 'And don't I have to get a wee cheque from you before I trap for Glasgow?'

'Excuse me,' Miller said. 'Back in a minute.' He got to his feet and left the office.

Campbell kept his eyes fixed on the television screen, where the cat and the mouse in the cartoon were eating food from the same bowl. The cat was encouraging the mouse to nibble at a morsel of food. The mouse thanked the cat fulsomely, and even though he did, in a jump–cut the cat seized hold of the mouse in a furry fist and brought him up to his mouth as though he were going to eat him. Campbell could not make out the dialogue between them as the volume control was set too low, but it was clear to him that the big cat would not get his own way for too long and that the mouse would have another trick in his repertoire of evasive moves and would not be subservient for much longer.

Miller entered holding a cheque and a contract in his right hand. 'Right, Donald, sign this contract, and I'll sign the cheque.'

There was a half minute of silence as both men occupied themselves with writing.

Miller extended the cheque towards Campbell and took the contract from him. 'You've had a profitable journey,' he said.

'It's at the end of the game,' Campbell said, 'we find out who's made a profit.'

'What does that mean?'

'Just that we've only taken the first step today.'

'Aren't you the old sage! What's the matter with you? It's only television.'

'I know it's only television,' Campbell said, 'and I'd very much like to be part of that.'

'You try and get on top of this treatment, Donald,' Miller said, 'and – who knows? – maybe there'll be the odd bit of work for you now and again. Would you like to work in here?'

'No thanks. I'd go off my head if I had to spend the whole week in here.'

'How's that?'

'All those television sets,' Campbell said, a broad grin on his face. 'I've never in all my life seen so many television sets in one place. You've even got one in the toilet!'

'That's right. What's wrong with that? That's the business we're in.'

'I know,' Campbell said, 'but they left me terribly confused today. There I was in the gents', having a crafty smoke, staring like a pre-schooler at *Tom and Jerry*. Then the adverts came on. I came into your office, and I was so turned about, I almost did my *dileag* on your desk.'

Miller laughed dutifully. 'I'll let you trap with your *lowie*,' he said, extending his hand. He did not get out of his chair. 'Enjoyed your visit.'

'Me, too,' Campbell said. 'Thanks for giving me a shot at this new work.' He turned and walked out the door.

50

Miller kept his eyes fixed on Campbell until he closed the door behind him on his way out of the Albion Television headquarters. Finally, convinced that Campbell could not possibly overhear him, he lifted the phone and punched in numbers.

7

The young Turkish dancer removed the scarf from around Campbell's neck when the lively Middle Eastern music on the CD player came to an end. She placed it around her own shoulders, covering her bosom, and she thanked him and a dozen other diners in the Bosphorus Restaurant on St George's Road in Glasgow on Sunday evening by flashing a mouthful of large, very white teeth at everybody. Campbell stood in the middle of the dining room where she had been swaying and writhing, half naked, before enfolding his neck in folds of silk, and making him perform a kind of Turkish reel along with her. He inclined his head and bowed towards the people who were still eating at little tables round the dance floor. He clapped his hands in appreciation of the young woman's performance and smiled at her before returning to his own table in the corner.

George Kerr, seated in a chair next to his, extended his right hand. 'You had a real Turkish delight there, Donald. Wouldn't she make a delightful wee present for somebody who's been busy all day in the library?'

'Hi, George,' Campbell said, 'made any good programmes lately?'

'You know yourself,' Kerr said. 'Some half decent. Some not so good. I hope to make a cracker along with you very soon – *Cuid do Chroinn*.'

'How,' Campbell asked, 'did you find me?'

'Your girl,' Kerr answered, 'told me where you'd be.'

'My girl?' Campbell said.

'Yeah,' Kerr said, 'tall, blonde, lives above the Islander in Govan. Said you'd be in the Mitchell all day. Preparing for *Cuid do Chroinn*, were you?'

'Something like that,' Campbell said.

'And,' Kerr said, 'aren't you doing some work for John Alex, too?'

'Oh,' Campbell said, 'that job might never come to anything. I think I've pulled the pin on that one.'

'What's the reason?' Kerr said.

'Well,' Campbell said, 'I found a better job. I mean, I thought at the time I'd found a better job.'

'What are you up to now?' Kerr said.

'You'll hardly believe this,' Campbell said. 'I'm thinking of going back on the road again.'

'Never,' Kerr said. 'I thought you'd given the elbow to that kind of work. How long since you did your last gig – six months?'

'Week last Friday,' Campbell said. 'Did a favour for a pal of mine over in Govan. I was out of practice and I thought I'd do a wee live gig before going to Perth to record *Cuid do Chroinn*.'

'Tell me truthfully, Donald,' Kerr said, 'are you looking forward to *Cuid do Chroinn*?'

'Yes,' Campbell said.

'Me, too,' Kerr said. 'And it's going to be a great programme. I'm going to make sure of that. I've produced over a hundred and fifty programmes of *Take a Chance* in

English, and I'm going to tell you this: the man who's in the driving seat for this first series will have a glorious future in television.' He snapped his fingers at the Turkish girl who, in Versace jeans and a white blouse buttoned up to the neck, was now serving the other tables. He ordered two Turkish coffees and turned back to Campbell. 'I hope, Donald, you will be that man.'

'I don't understand,' Campbell said.

'Listen,' Kerr said. 'Just after New Year, that half-wit at Iomhaigh Productions gave you two and a half thousand pounds. Well, he gave the money to West End Travel and I've discovered you collected tickets and travellers' cheques to go to Venezuela. That came all together to round about fourteen hundred pounds, and they wrote you a cheque for a little over eleven hundred pounds. Here's the bottom line: unless you repay that money, we'll initiate legal action against you and we'll get somebody else to do *Cuid do Chroinn.*'

'I think,' Campbell said, 'I understand you now.' He attempted to smile at the girl who brought the coffees.

They both looked at the girl's rump and her long, black, wavy hair as she walked on dancer's feet away from their table.

'Donald,' Kerr said, 'we're not going to fall out over this, are we?'

'No,' Campbell said, still gazing at the girl as she stacked dishes on a tray at the far end of the room.

'Did you see anything as gorgeous as her,' Kerr asked, 'when you were over there?'

'Scores,' Campbell said.

'I believe it,' Kerr said. 'Seems that you appeal to the women, Donald. I think the Turkish chick fancies you.'

'No,' Campbell said. 'She's a grafter, and she tries to be pleasant. And I like that. Because I'm the exact same with the ladies. I put myself out to please them. As far as I'm concerned, anyway, there's no other way.'

'Our friend Maclean,' Kerr said, 'has an eye for the women, too, hasn't he?'

'Certainly has,' Campbell said. 'But there's a difference. Women don't like him at all. They sense that he isn't really fond of them – that all he wants from them is sex. He doesn't respect them. And the women know he's like that.'

'Don't you like him?' Kerr asked.

'He deserves praise,' Campbell said, 'for how well he's done – you know, like getting into television with so little natural talent.'

'You don't think too much, then,' Kerr said, 'of his intellectual prowess? A man who attained the rank of university professor at the age of thirty-five?'

'Put it this way,' Campbell said, 'the only job in television John Alex would be fit for would be answering the telephone when folk ask what time *News at Ten* starts.'

Kerr almost choked on his coffee. He reached for a silk handkerchief, but before he could put it to his mouth the Turkish girl was at his side offering a paper napkin. Kerr wiped his chin and the cuffs of his shirt. 'How charming of her!' he said. 'She looks lovely, too.'

'She wouldn't stand a chance,' Campbell said, 'against Mercedes.'

56

Kerr gave a crooked smile. 'You'd better tell me all about it, then.'

'Might as well,' Campbell said. 'Well, I collected the plane tickets and the travellers' cheques, right? And a personal cheque made out to me for eleven hundred pounds. I was – I almost said I was feeling terrific, but it was better than that – I was absolutely ecstatic the way things were. We left Heathrow on Saturday morning, and I was sipping away at rum and Cokes all during the flight. I had a nice glow on when we touched down in Caracas, and because we had to stay in the airport before boarding a plane to Isla Margarita, I saw nothing better than to bounce into the bar and order two or three additional Cuba Libres. I wasn't drunk, know what I mean? I wasn't rubbered, but heat and fatigue were closing in on me, so when we reached the island I was snoring away at the back of the plane. My watch was telling me it was five o'clock in the afternoon, but it was much later than that. However, the girls who worked for the airline were terribly sweet, and I was deposited on the tarmac with little delay. In one bound, Donald was in a taxi heading for a hotel in the island capital.

'Anyway, I drank a miniature of rum that had been left out for me in the room, I bought a hundred pounds' worth of bolivares and I took a stroll downtown to get a bite to eat. I was famished.

'I saw this bar – I still remember the name: Cantina Caribe – down by the port and I went in. Now, you've got to understand how things are in that country. First of all, out of all the newly born babies in Venezuela the vast majority of them are female. We don't know why this should be so. But it's true. Women make up two thirds of the population, perhaps even more. Second of all, they're very pretty, these women. They're mixtures of every shade – some with black skins, others as fair as Swedes, and the remainder every shade in between. The people are extremely proud of their womenfolk. They'll tell you that entrants from Venezuela have taken home the title of Miss World more times than any other nation. I don't know if this is true, but I personally believe them. The young women over there are exceptionally lovely. And there's a lot of them about. And just because, perhaps, they're so numerous they're very friendly. Perhaps over-friendly, I think now, towards an old man from *Gearradh na Mòna*.

'Well, whatever. I was waiting for the fajitas, and I decided, like, you know, that I should order another glass of brandy. I felt as though there were no bones in my body. But the waitress was terribly nice – Marta her name was – and she was keen that I should take her phone number down, you know, if I felt lonely, and all I had to do was give her a call, and she'd come to my hotel right away.

'Oh, I know fine what you're thinking. But you're wrong. I didn't accept her invitation at all. Well, anyway, I didn't there and then. I ate my meal, and I really enjoyed their food. And – you don't have to ask – I drank a whole rake of other brandies as well. Paid the bill, left a tip for Marta and took a taxi back to the hotel.

'According to my watch, it was now round about eleven o'clock, half past eleven – something like that – when I made it back to the hotel. I considered there was no harm

58

in having a bottle of beer before going up to my room. There was a bar beside the swimming pool. I sat down and ordered a bottle of Sol. Juan Luis Guerra was singing on the tape – "Como Abeja Al Panal" – and there was a woman accompanying him the likes of which I'd never heard in all my life. I was completely made up. This was really flying. There was a full moon and a fair crowd of folk sitting beneath the palm trees chattering away in Spanish, drinking and smoking.

'That was when,' Campbell said, 'I made my first mistake.'

'What,' Kerr enquired, 'did you do?'

'I started to have a conversation with the young guy who was working behind the bar. That's what I did. "Okay, young man," I said, "*¿tiene usted Scotch?*"

' "Scotch whi'ky?" Their dialect tends to be a bit lispy over there, know what I mean? Well, it wasn't long before yours truly here was just as lispy and stuttery as them. I started on Johnnie Walker Red Label, the stuff they bottle themselves over there though it comes in bulk from our country. I was half in the bag by this time and I didn't notice the odd couple who were sitting at a wrought-iron table nearby.

' "*Mira, la rubia,*" the young guy says, and I saw this tall blonde girl, nothing on but a skimpy bikini. She had blonde hair certainly, but you knew she had Negro blood somewhere in her genetic endowment. She couldn't have been more than eighteen years of age. But what turned me about completely was that she had along with her an ugly old guy with his arm tight round her waist. And this guy was really ugly. He was a kind of tiny little gnome, completely bald with one or two rotting stumps in his head.

' "*¿Qué pasa?*" I said to the young guy, anxious to find out how this gorgeous young thing ended up with a wizened old prune who'd scare the life out of you.

' "*Ella es una puta*," the young guy says, and I sensed that I was about to have a memorable night. I had no idea how good she was going to be. But I knew this much: that I'd never forget her. No, indeed. "A prostitute," says I. "*¿Cuanto costeria por la noche?*" What'll she cost, all night?

' "*No mucho*," the young guy says. "*Cuatrocientos bolivares. ¿Quieres*, four hundred bolivares. You like?"

'And I said: "No, no, no." But I was lying – to him and to myself. Hey, just over two pounds to have sex with a creature like that? I made up my mind, in an instant, to stop thinking about it and just do it.

' "*¿Puedo llamar por teléfono de aquí?*" I says to the young guy.' Campbell shrugged as though in apology. 'And that's how I hooked up with Marta, and after my humiliation with her, made the sweet acquaintance of the blonde negress Mercedes.'

'Was she worth it?' Kerr asked.

'Naw,' Campbell replied. 'I was drunk. Totally my own fault. I'm not worth a curdie to a woman when I'm Baltic. It's happened before, and I'm sure it'll happen again. All I can remember about the rest of the night is opening a bottle of whi'ky upstairs while I waited for Marta. I was fast asleep on the sofa when she phoned from reception downstairs. I let her in. Things were pretty hazy. I recall being seated at the foot of the bed in the *dormitorio* and feeling totally smashed. She was standing in front of me and she did something that filled me with wonder. She yanked the collar of her dress down to one side exposing one exquisite breast. With one hand she held the breast pointing proudly towards me, gripped the back of my neck with her other hand and gently ferried my head forward. She sang as she tenderly stroked the back of my head. I could hear "*Cada vez que me abrazas*" – and never in all my life have I experienced a kiss as natural as that.'

'Did you,' Kerr asked, 'you know, have sex with her?'

'No,' Campbell replied, and his voice grew hoarse. 'I let on I'd drunk too much and couldn't sleep with her. I remember she laughed when I illustrated with a dangling forefinger how my old man remained obdurately soft. But do you know this, George? That was just an excuse. I wanted to go with her. But I felt somehow I wasn't worthy of her, know what I mean? That wasn't Donald Campbell she had that night, but a cowardly old man who was so unsure of himself that he had to get plastered to even think about going to bed with a woman. I was awash in an ocean of shame. Then, I became angry: not at her – with myself, know what I mean? I dived under the blanket and ordered her to leave. "*Necesito poco dinero – voy tomar un taxi*," she says. I said, "*Aquí es mi cartera*." And I handed her my wallet. What a bampot – the thing stuffed with money and travellers' cheques! When I think back to that night, I'm convinced that part of me wanted what happened to me actually to happen.'

'What was that?' Kerr asked.

'She went off with my money,' Campbell said. 'I was feeling so guilty at taking drink – despite all the promises I'd made in my life never to do that again. I was . . . I think I was trying to punish myself. And the strange thing about all this is: I don't know to this day if she stole the money or if I lost it after she'd gone. I came to in the morning on the sofa in the *sala* surrounded by a pile of cans and bottles. I must have gone downstairs to the bar again, but, honestly, I can't tell you for sure what happened after I sent Marta packing.

'Anyway, I clearly remember the following day, though. I've never spent such an awful day in all my life. Head was leaking, I was as dry as a cork and I didn't have a sun-tanned two pence piece on me to buy even an orange juice. I stayed beside the swimming pool all day. Now and again, I'd leap into the water just to cool my lips. Little kids had taken over the pool and their screeching was doing my box in.

'I was up in my room that night, hanging up my gear before going down to the dining room where I'd maybe get something to drink. This was about ten o'clock and I was absolutely parched. I was folding the shirt I'd worn when leaving the UK, when I felt some kind of folded paper object in the breast pocket. This was the cheque the guy in the travel agent's had written for me two days previously. That's me out the traps like Usain Bolt and down the stairs to see Señor Mendez, the old guy who changed money for you at reception. No sign of him. When I showed the cheque to the other members of staff on duty, they looked at me as though I'd indecently propositioned them.

62

"*Mañana por la mañana*," they said. And I kept repeating I couldn't wait until the morning. Finally, one of the girls said that the only one who might be able to help me was Mercedes. And who was Mercedes? Who but the blonde negress I'd seen with the old man the previous night.

'Nothing else for it but to go to the booth next door where she was employed selling tat to the tourists. She examined the cheque and we chatted back and forth, and at last she said she'd exchange it for Venezuelan bolivares. But she would have to go to Porlamar to meet with a friend who'd be able to carry out the transaction. My dusky saviour left in a taxi clutching my precious wee cheque and Donald the Dunce sat scrunched up on a sofa by the door of the shop, *eating* cigarettes, one after another. She left about eleven and came back about one in the morning. Two hours, or two weeks it seemed, after taking off. What a welcome I gave her when she waltzed in with a bundle of bolivares in her hand!'

'I know what happened next,' Kerr said. 'The pair of you got smashed together and then went back to your room, right?'

'No, we didn't,' Campbell said, 'and we didn't go upstairs together either. It's hard to believe, but I didn't touch a drop that night. I thanked Mercedes, bought a dozen cans of Coke and went up to my room. By myself.

'The next day, I didn't touch the booze either. I stayed by the swimming pool all day and did a fair bit of sweating. When the kids' screaming got too much for me, I'd toddle upstairs for a slug of Coke. One time I looked in at the restaurant where they were holding Spanish language

63

lessons. Remember, this was the second day of my vacation, and I was on the point of going off my head. People were getting on my nerves as well. Big, fat, hairy men with water-wings splashing about in the pool, and old, leathery hags applying sun lotion on their wrinkled bodies. Everywhere I turned someone was causing me offence. Even the waiters, they disgusted me the way they strutted about juggling their bottles of mineral water. I thought: "God be round about you, Donald, you've spent better nights than this in Back." But, as usual, I was wrong again. The way things worked out, I had a night out in Porlamar the likes of which I've never had, or for that matter nobody in the Poligan – that's a row of houses in Back – has ever had.

'What happened was, Mercedes came over to my table. "Hola, Papa," she says, "may I have a beer, please?" And I'm telling you, George, no one could have denied her. I went over to the counter and ordered a little dumpy bottle of lager for her – Polar it was called – and a glass of fresh orange for me. "*¿Cuánto es?*" says she, asking me what I'd paid for her drink. I told her and she burst out laughing. "*Las bebidas están incluidas,*" she says. The drinks were free!

'Well, when I thought of how I'd been suffering all day, I was really angry at my stupidity, and that's when the drinking began. It wasn't very heavy at first. With my ebony goddess opposite me inflaming my senses with her long, smooth black thighs only inches away from my knees and her almost exposed breasts about to poke me in the eye, it was no contest. "*Vamos a bailar,*" she says, inviting me to go with her to a disco in the capital. I quickly waved the white flag of surrender and I didn't just run, I jumped. Why should I stay in my own hotel where I could have all I could drink absolutely free, when I could make a clown of myself in company that'd possibly be quite dangerous and where I'd be able to spend a fortune on watered-down drinks? In with the head down. Off we go in a taxi to Porlamar. As far as I can tell, we had a splendid night – don't ask, George, I don't know if it was Mercedes who saw me home. But *somebody* must have seen me home, because I surfaced in my own room in the hotel and the place was a tip – bottles of rum, boxes of cigars and cigarettes, chocolate boxes, clothes scattered all over the floor.'

'How were you feeling?' Kerr said.

'Powerful. Just a wee tad dry. And that didn't last long. I got stuck into the bottles of Polar that were left, took a cold shower, threw on shorts and a T-shirt and ran down the stairs to Big Mercedes' shop. After a couple of rums there I felt so bold as to ask her to take the day off and come for a picnic with me down by the beach. And that's how I carried on nearly every day. I never drew a sober breath for three weeks. And I didn't spare the wallet either. I bought gold rings for us, a camera for me, and an expensive watch for her, tropical gear for us both – I lost the plot completely.

'Never mind though, in the words of the Blind Harpist, "As the wheel turns, so the warmth turned to chill." Wow, and how! On the last day of my sordid little flight from reality I was so much the worse the wear on account of the drink – I was drinking whisky by the poolside bar and quivering like a fishing rod – when this fellow from Edinburgh came up to me and put his arms round my shoulder. He and his wife were guests in the place and had been watching me gradually coming apart for all of three weeks. All he said was: "Time to go back to bonnie Scotland, pal. Come on, we'll give you a hand with your stuff." I got up from the stool with some difficulty, kissed Mercedes and with nothing in my trouser pocket but my passport and my flight tickets, bade farewell to the hotel, Venezuela and its womenfolk.

'On the flight back I thought about bailing out a few times, I was feeling so depressed and guilty. But I managed to finish the best part of a litre of white rum, and I slept like a stone for the best part of the way. When I arrived in Glasgow with only a wee cotton shirt, shorts and flip–flops on, I jumped a taxi to my sister's house in Partick, and I remained under the duvet for almost a week before I was able to keep any food down.' He sighed. 'And that, George, is the connection between Mercedes and two and a half grand.'

'Why don't you make up your mind never to go near the stuff again?' Kerr said.

'Och, I've done that loads of times,' Campbell said. 'But now I think that's the underlying problem. I've been so focused on avoiding the stuff that as soon as I take a drop I try to drown myself in it. But I've a new notion I've been developing for a while, since I came back from Venezuela, actually. Very gradually I've come to embrace the idea that if I'm going to be abstinent, I must welcome . . . umh, *joy* into my life. I've been awestruck by the ongoing, interminable wrangle between me and drug alcohol. The stuff's not like King Cowell or Queen Cheryl, you know, shiny lives that'll soon tarnish. No, the stuff's more popular than Coca-Cola. All I have to do on a daily basis is remove myself from the debating chamber. I've been paralysed by fear of the battle for too long.'

'Well, you paid dearly for your trip, Donald. Two and a half grand. Ouch! When can I expect a cheque from you?'

'Tell you what I'll do,' Campbell said. 'I'll give you five hundred now and I'll send you the balance before the end of the month.'

'No way. I can't accept five hundred. Up your offer.'

'How about,' Campbell said, 'I give you one thousand pounds just now and fifteen hundred a week tomorrow?'

A beat. 'Very well,' Kerr said, 'and we'll leave it at that.'

Campbell took the chequebook out and began to write. To the Turkish girl who had materialised beside them like a ghost he said, 'My uncle George's paying for the meal. Very keen on exotic women is our George.'

8

As he sat at the table along with Gus Miller and Carol Macleod of Albion Television in Chez Maurice, an up-market French restaurant near Picardy Place in Edinburgh, Campbell worried that the food Miller had ordered for the three of them might not appeal to a rather sulky-faced Carol. From the corner of one eye he watched her taking a full half minute to spread butter on a piece of garlic bread while he and Miller were already chewing away. They all had the same dish – scallops fried in butter with wraps of bacon and raw onions. 'Do try these scallops, dear,' Campbell said to Carol. 'This is a lovely meal, Gus. Thank you for inviting me.'

Miller tucked his green Hermes tie in between the top two buttons of his pink cotton shirt to avoid dripping butter on it and laughed. 'Thank you, Donald,' he said. 'I really enjoyed that piece you wrote . . . Immensely, man – by the way, did you get the cheque from Elaine?'

'Yes, I did, thanks,' Campbell said absentmindedly as he tried to work out what Carol had paid for the forest green John Galliano trouser suit and the Jimmy Choo six-inch heels she was wearing. He turned towards her. 'I thought, Carol,' he said, 'you wanted to talk to me about some project or other you're conducting in your department. What do you have in mind?'

She did not respond. Carefully she raised her fork and placed a pierced slice of scallop on her tongue. Campbell noticed that the gloss on her lips had grown faint and would soon require another application of balm. Her brow seemed greasy as well, and Campbell guessed she had not had enough time to powder her face before coming to the restaurant. Despite that, she didn't seem to be in any hurry to tell him why the three of them were dining in the most expensive restaurant in the capital.

'Donald,' Miller said, 'how'd you fancy doing a wee night in the Camus Leisure Centre in Fort William?'

'I'd quite fancy that,' Campbell said.

'Of course,' Miller said, 'you'd have backing – musicians, a female singer, dancers, folk like that. What we want is for you to put together a . . . er, hunting party, as it were, from the South. You'd have an outside broadcast van with an experienced director and shooting crew and support team for two days. You'd go up to the heart of North Television territory. You'll hose down the entire show– you, Donald, will have sole artistic responsibility for front-of-camera action. We'll edit the tapes down here in our own edit suite and we'll maybe get two half-hour programmes out of the exercise.'

'Three,' Carol Macleod said.

'Right,' Miller said. 'Who would you like to go along with you, Donald? Could MacAskill hack it?'

'I reckon he could,' Campbell said. 'Wouldn't cost much anyway.'

'How cheap could we get him for?' Carol Macleod said.

'He'll take a hundred notes,' Campbell said.

'Who'd be along with him,' Miller said, 'in the band?'

'Well,' Campbell said, 'he'd want Big John on drums with him for sure, and it'll be easy enough to get someone to play guitar. Doesn't have to be Clapton: just as long as he owns an instrument. I'd play guitar myself, if you're trying to save money.'

'We most certainly are,' Carol Macleod said.

'I'd never have guessed,' Campbell said.

'We try to save money,' Carol Macleod said, 'at all times.'

'Okay,' Miller broke in, 'let's say you and MacAskill and somebody else from the back line for the "Dance to Follow" thingy. Who would you want as female vocalist at the concert bit?'

'Mary MacLennan,' Campbell said.

'Oh, right,' Miller said. 'That's the pretty brunette who fronted those children's programmes for the Beeb, right? She's nice and sexy. What do you think, Carol?'

'Dyes her hair and she's too tall to be sexy,' Carol Macleod said. 'Important thing is – what'll we have to pay her by way of a fee?'

'Well,' Campbell said, 'the evening would fall into three parts, I think, and Mary would appear three times, singing three or four songs each time. All in, she'd be covering about a dozen numbers.'

'I repeat my question,' Carol Macleod said. 'What would she charge?'

'As I've been trying to explain,' Campbell said, 'if she's going to be on as often as that, she'll want a cenny and a half at least. She wouldn't do a heavy night like that for you lot, but she'll maybe do me a favour.'

Miller cleared his throat. 'Tell me, Donald, what'll you be doing? Piping, I'm sure. You still singing? Oh aye, you'll surely be doing those characters of yours – the thick policeman from Uist and the drunken steamer skipper from Barra . . . Oh, and the elder, is that right?'

'It'll be a right poke of Dolly Mixtures,' Campbell said, 'know what I mean? The pipes, of course, to open and close: a wee while at the singing, then a wee tune or two on flute or clarinet, and the rest of the time telling lies and trying to get strangers to laugh.'

'Hey, it's looking good already,' Miller said. He turned to Carol Macleod. 'What do you think, Carol?'

Macleod raised her head. The pupils of her eyes were greatly enlarged and she ran her tongue over her lips before speaking. 'Here's the deal I'm offering you,' she said. 'The Camus Centre will be full that night. We'll make sure of that. Over the coming three weeks we'll plant items singing your praises in the press and radio. On the night there'll be six hundred folk in the centre, and there'll be a hefty admission charge.' She raised her hand palm outwards. 'Oh, I don't know – say a fiver a skull. The management and I have already come to an agreement. They'll get twenty per cent of all revenues, and the remaining eighty will be divided between you and Albion. Should come out at just under two and a half grand. You get a grand. Satisfied?'

'No,' Campbell said.

'Why not?' Carol Macleod said.

'There was no mention of . . . you didn't specify a fee for the television programmes you're going to make from the footage.'

'The result of every game,' Carol said, 'comes at the end. We'll give you six hundred pounds for each programme. It'll be up to you to pay the musos and the brunette out of your end. Nevertheless, unless my arithmetic's faulty, you'll have . . . wait a second . . . you'll have nearly three thousand pounds to play with.'

Campbell put his fork down, lifted his napkin and wiped his mouth. 'Hold it right there, girl. In the first place, I can't remember when you and I got married. I think I would've recollected something like that, you being so pretty and all. But when you were doing your rap just then, I was doing my damnedest to remember when exactly we got together. And – isn't it strange? – I can't remember the wedding reception, the marriage ceremony or even the first night of the honeymoon. How low has the bevy brought me! I'll really have to pull the pin on those drams. I'll get to the point: we never did get married. I'm a freelancer. If I fancy doing a wee concert in Fort William, or anywhere in the Highlands for that matter, I'll organise the concert myself. Whatever we make at the door, the manager'll get twenty per cent and the rest will be mine. Wouldn't have to be a packer for me to score around two grand. Two thousand for Donald Campbell, you understand? And what's for sure, I won't have a greedy wife waiting with her hand out for half of it.' He took a deep breath and moved his head from side to side. 'In the second place, Carol, even if I had agreed to share a bed with you, I'd be a laughing stock, a source of shame and an object of pity if I agree to the fee you mentioned. Six hundred pounds for the supporting cast! Excluding expenses! And Albion getting three programmes from it!'

'We'll be giving you,' Miller said, 'a fee of eighteen hundred pounds.'

'Six hundred quid to cover each programme?' Campbell said. 'You're far too low. Before I'd even get a van and petrol to go into it, before I'd pay for lodgings and food, before paying local dancers, and after I'd paid Calum Iain and Big John and Mairi, I'd have to – I'd need to spend four hundred and fifty pounds, at least. Any money left over for me would be a joke.

'And another thing,' he continued, looking directly into Carol Macleod's eyes, 'why are you so mean with your own people, Carol? I'd expect to meet tight-fisted pricks among the Lowlanders, but I never thought I'd come across someone so cheap who comes from the parish of Lochs.'

'Be careful, Donald,' Miller said. 'Watch your mouth.'

'Leave him alone, Gus,' Carol Macleod said. 'Donald, I hope you believe me when I say I feel sorry for you. To us in Albion Television there is no distinction made between Lowlander and Gael. Some of our Gaelic language programmes we fund ourselves and others receive financial assistance from the STG. The money for both streams comes from the same reservoir and – you've got to understand this, Donald – our reservoir is drying up. We're challenged by lack of money in the economy, a diminution in advertising revenue and much larger and more powerful companies in the South are threatening to gobble us up. That's why we're "mean" towards you and everybody else who works for us.

'I'm going to tell you a wee story, Donald,' she continued. 'Listen carefully. We had a vacancy last week for a presenter in the news department. Know how many young graduates, of both genders, applied for it? Let me enlighten you. One hundred and seventy-nine. And do you know what we were offering as a yearly salary? Wait for it: nineteen thousand.' She raised her hand as though to stifle Campbell before he had opened his mouth. 'Let me finish my little speech. We're in an intensely competitive business. This is neither a pastime nor a hobby. Let it be clear in your mind that we at Albion Television are going to put a show on in the Camus Centre in Fort William in three and a half weeks' time, whether you're with us or not. If you're dissatisfied with the package, don't take it. What we'll do is, we'll get one of our male trainees and we'll write out all his dialogue on idiot boards – we'll not even hire an autocue operator for a couple of hours – and he'll parrot all his lines, even if it takes seventeen takes for each speech, directly to camera with a big grin on his face. I now know who'll be playing and singing – oh, I'll pick up a young male vocalist for buttons at the RSAMD – and I know what fees they'll accept. Make your mind up time, Donald.'

'I can't . . .' Campbell began. 'I won't be bullied like this. You can't do that.'

'We can,' Miller said. 'You gave us your advice for nothing, and we're going to use it.'

'It wasn't really free,' Carol Macleod said, 'the advice he gave us, Gus. Aren't Albion paying for his meal?' And she resumed eating.

Campbell crumpled his napkin and placed it beside the plate which still contained food. 'Wait a minute, Carol. Maybe I was a wee bit hasty there.'

'I'll give you exactly thirty seconds, Donald,' Carol Macleod said, 'to make a decision. Make up your mind. Are you going to do it or not?'

'Okay,' Campbell said. 'I agree. But won't you reconsider the money?'

'I already have done,' Carol Macleod said. 'I've changed my mind. I've decided to reduce your fee to one thousand seven hundred. From the money we make at the door, you'll get a third of that. That's after we weigh-in the management at the Camus Centre.' She stopped talking and gave him a flash of lipstick-stained teeth. 'What's the matter, Donald? Why don't you finish your scallops?'

'I've kind of lost my appetite,' Campbell said.

'You take what he's left, Gus,' Carol Macleod said to Miller. 'We're paying for it anyway, aren't we?'

'That's right, Carol,' Gus Miller said as he deftly whipped Campbell's plate over to his place setting. 'We'd better not let good food go to waste when we've already paid for it.' He extended his right hand to an astounded Donald Campbell. 'Welcome to Albion Television, Donald. Stick with us, kid, and there's no knowing how far you'll reach.'

'I'm afraid I've reached the end of the road already,' Campbell said. 'I've been hearing about *Taigh nam Bochd*, the House of the Poor, all my life, and, finally, I've arrived in it.' He waved his arm in an expansive gesture, taking in the acres of velvet, Italian leather and starched linen. 'But I'd no idea it'd look so lovely.'

9

'Where is he?' George Kerr said to Duncan Sinclair in the Iomhaigh Productions office at midday. 'Don't tell me the titular head of this company has gone to Stornoway again to confer with our Flora.'

'He went to Ireland,' Sinclair said as his fingers drummed on the computer keyboard. 'You know, to that big Celtic festival in Dublin. Left yesterday by plane.'

'I don't know,' Kerr said, shaking his head. 'Why do have the feeling it's me who'll be paying for this further down the line?'

'You can ask him tomorrow why he left in such a hurry. He said something to me about a company like Iomhaigh having to go in for co-production, but I was on the phone at the time and I didn't pay much attention to what he said. This was yesterday morning, and he wasn't in for long. He didn't even sit down.'

'When do you expect him?'

'They're coming back tomorrow afternoon.'

Kerr scowled. 'They?'

'John Alex and Donna,' Sinclair said.

'Who is Donna?'

Sinclair pressed a button on his computer, closed the lid and inhaled deeply. 'Donna MacIver is a Lewis woman,' he said. 'That is, she's a young girl from the Point district of Lewis. John Alex and her brother were fairly pally once upon a time. They were at university together. He's a solicitor now.'

'I don't give a fig what he is,' Kerr said. 'What is she?'

'Well,' Sinclair said, smiling, 'she's a good-looking young bird. She's – how to put this delicately? – she's a gorgeously well put-together young bird. She'll be about, I'd guess – I'm about ten years older than her, and I'm twenty-eight, and so, if I were to guess her age, I'd have to say she's . . .'

'Young,' Kerr said. 'You know, Duncan, every time I wonder why you got the bullet from the Beeb, you always remind me of the reason.'

'Okay, she's just left the Nicolson Institute in Stornoway, she wants to get any kind of job in television, she wears too much make-up and she doesn't wear a bra. Is that good enough for you?'

'No,' Kerr said, 'that's not good enough. We have a series of television programmes to make in a month's time, and the head of the company's off on a jolly to Ireland, a trip I've paid for, along with a . . . well, *bimbo*.' He lifted up a pile of papers on the desk and glanced through them. 'What have you been up to?'

'Personal letters,' Sinclair said, 'to the folk who're going to be in the studio when we record the programmes, you know, thanking them for agreeing to take part, contracts to the contestants and the team leaders – boring stuff, you understand, but very necessary, I think. Oh, I've been doing some . . . er, creative work, too, trying to polish two or three ideas I've had for other programmes.'

'What other programmes?'

'They're not finished yet,' Sinclair said, 'but you can take a look at them, see if they're any good.' He handed over a plump plastic folder. 'There's a historical documentary in there about the Sobieski Stolberg Stuart brothers, another about witchcraft in the islands, one about hidden treasure in locations throughout the West Highlands and there's a passing reference to further game shows. These are the kind of programmes that might appeal to North Television if they'd agree to be the broadcasters.'

Kerr carefully shuffled the papers and replaced them in the folder. 'Listen, Duncan, do you, ah, do you get a lot of these ideas coming to you? Another thing I meant to ask you as well: who chose Campbell for *Cuid do Chroinn*? Was it John Alex who thought of him first?'

'Well, to tell you the truth,' Sinclair said, 'John Alex didn't really know about Campbell before I put his name up for consideration for the presenter's job. Me, I was always a keen fan from a young age. I can still remember a series of programmes he made for the Beeb fifteen years ago – *Who Else But Campbell?* was the title, and everybody in Barra was square-eyed watching it – which turned out to be a phenomenon in the realm of Gaelic light entertainment. He's a genuinely funny guy. And folk like that are scarce nowadays.'

'Maybe you're right,' Kerr said. 'Does Maclean think he's funny?'

'I don't know,' Sinclair said. 'The kind of man he is, it's hard to tell. You can never know for sure what he's thinking. He's, like, inscrutable.'

81

'Nonsense!' Kerr said. 'We all know what he's thinking. His brains are in his groin.'

'Campbell calls him "the Mountie",' Kerr said. 'Says Maclean's like a Mountie, only he doesn't have a horse. I get scared at times that John Alex will hear some of the things Campbell says about him when he's slagging him off. You should've heard him the other day when we were chatting in here, me and Donald, about next month's programmes. He was telling me how he'd warm up the audience while he was off camera during the show. You know how English variety programmes always employed warm-up acts to enable the director to get reaction shots of the audience having a good time. Any time you saw the faces of the audience at a televised ceilidh on Gaelic television, he claimed, everybody looked as though their collie dogs had been run over by a tractor. I said, "That'll be fine by me, Donald, but I'm only the dogsbody in this company. You'd better hold on until John Alex comes in."'

'Professor John Alex Maclean is to be the arbiter of good humour?' Kerr said. 'How did Campbell respond to that?'

'Well,' Sinclair said, 'he just sniggered and said, "Dismiss John Alex from your mind, Duncan. If it wasn't for his friendship with Gordon Anderson at North Television he's be selling the *Big Issue* on the streets. And he'd be happy doing that. He could then start boasting he was in journalism. 'Get your *Big Issue* here, folks. Check it out. Check it out.' The man's porch light fused a long time ago, Duncan. Oh, he's certainly got stamina. But we have machines nowadays to cut our peat for us. Forget about

John Alex, my man. The old Prof's gone out of fashion."
And the way he was talking, I honestly thought he
wouldn't have cared if John Alex had heard him. He
was as cocky as that.'

'He's certainly self-confident,' Kerr said. 'But that's no
bad thing for a guy who's going to present *Cuid do
Chroinn*.'

'I'm pleased to hear that,' Sinclair said. 'Does that mean
he's paid back the money?'

'No, he hasn't,' Kerr said. 'Well, he did give me a
cheque for a thousand and I've still to get the rest of it. But
we'll get it – you better believe it.'

'Well, I hope he gets the money and he'll be with us for
these programmes. Campbell's going to be terrific in *Cuid
do Chroinn*.'

'I'm hoping as well,' Kerr said, 'that he gets his hands
on a grand and a half. And I'm convinced, like you, he'll be
great on the programme. And that's something I couldn't
say about everybody we know. Worst-case scenario, unlike
your esteemed leader, Campbell would at least know when
the *News at Ten* goes out.' He chuckled softly at his own
joke.

10

Campbell explained to Calum Iain MacAskill that the budget was tight. 'If it wasn't that Albion are strapped for cash just now, I'd give you more, Calum Iain, do you understand?' he said. He was standing with his back to the cigarette machine in the saloon bar of a pub on the Paisley Road West called the Ben Lomond. At quarter to twelve on a Monday morning the place was not busy. 'Don't say it, Calum Iain,' Campbell said. 'I know what you're thinking – that it's a pretty poor payday I'm offering you. But there's nothing left – know what I mean? I'd like to give you more, truthfully. But I can't.'

'I'd like that, too,' MacAskill said. 'But for doing something that's going on telly! When's it going out, do you know? That makes things a bit different. Even if we're going to be on the box, as you say we will be, I'd have thought I'd get more than a hundred pounds for something like that.'

'Well, I think you would've got more, too. Aye, once upon a time. But on this occasion Albion are cutting back, and so we've got to cut back as well. A hundred notes, that's it. I don't have any more to pay you.'

'You didn't used to be as tight as this, Donald. You used to be as kind as a seagull. Know this? You were a better man when you were drinking.'

'I was more stupid,' Campbell said, 'when I was drinking. I got wise. I now understand we've got to save money.

85

And before you say STG and squillions of money, let me tell you a thing or two about the television industry today.

'Some of the programmes that Albion broadcast, they're made with their own money; others are produced with financial assistance from the STG. Look at it this way: the money for both streams, as it were, is coming from two different lochs. As one of the lochs gets smaller, the one filled with advertising money, the independent companies have to rely more and more on public monies like the Beeb licence fee and the government-funded millions that the STG services. All the TV companies are experiencing hard times just now because unemployment is so high and people are not spending, advertising revenue is contracting . . . Oh, the list goes on and on. The provincial companies like North and Albion are scared that bigger companies from England are going to take a run at them and they'll be gobbled up. That's what's making them so *spìogach* about fees. You see, it's a business, my boy, not a hobby. And there are lots of little problems confronting TV nowadays.'

MacAskill held out his palm. 'Right there, Donald. I don't care how hard-up the "media people" are. None of my business. Everybody's got problems. But my own problems are the ones that worry me most. If I went into M&S and picked up a pack of cotton socks from the carousel and started arguing with the checkout girl about the price, do you think I'd get the pack any cheaper? "Hello, my dear, I can see that the price of seven pounds fifty is clearly marked on the package, but I've a confession to make. I'm a bit borassic lint just now on account of the low prices these Spanish pirates are paying us for our velvet crabs, so, I was wondering if you'd sell the socks to me for . . . ah, I don't know . . . er, a pound. What do you say, pet?" I know what she'd say all right. "Check all hospital beds. Deranged person at large in gents' accessories. I repeat: check all hospital beds." They'd huckle me off to the asylum, man.'

'That's my boy!' Campbell said. 'I wish I'd given that answer to Carol Macleod and Gus Miller at our luncheon in Edinburgh. To look at you, I'd never have guessed you were so smart. Where were you a week today when I needed you?'

'Right here,' MacAskill said, 'waiting as patiently as I am today for you to put your hand in your pocket and buy me a glass.'

'Never mind that just now,' Campbell said. 'I'm in a terrible hurry. Will you go up to Fort William with us on the seventeenth of March? Come on, Calum Iain, I'm in a right jam.'

'Will I take Johnny with me?'

'Don't bother,' Campbell said. 'We'll manage with just the three of us.'

'Who's the third man?'

'It's not a man, it's a woman.'

'Who is it, then?'

'Mary MacLennan.'

'That's great,' MacAskill said. 'I really like Mary.'

'I know. That's why you're going to phone her right away and ask her to come with us. You do that for me, Calum Iain, and I'll put your fee up to a hundred and twenty. How do you fancy that?'

'That's fine.'

'And we'll use your van?' Campbell said.

'I saw that coming,' MacAskill said. 'What a crook you've become, Donald! What'll I offer Mary?'

'A hundred and thirty quid.'

'You surely don't mean that, Donald,' MacAskill said. 'Mary would follow the example of that American woman if I told her that. What was her name again? Bobbitt, was it? Took a knife to her man's crown jewels, so she did. Oh, no, I'm not going to tell her that's all you're offering her.'

'Look here!' Campbell said. 'The pair of you are going to leave me bankrupt. Before I earn a penny for myself, I'm down two hundred and fifty already.'

'And you'll have to pay for the petrol, too.'

'Och, I give up,' Campbell said. 'You win. I hate this haggling over fees the way we're doing. Look, give her a bell, mate. Tell her I'll be extremely grateful.'

'I'll do it anyway,' MacAskill said, 'but I'm not all that confident that'll be enough.'

'See if you can talk her round,' Campbell said. He raised his eyes to the ceiling. 'I imagine I can still hear my poor old mother preaching to me. "The only thing, Donald, that will come between you and the Creator, will be other people taking advantage of your kindness." And I don't think the old lady was far wrong. Tell Mary I'll go to two hundred and – stuff it! – I'll give you a hundred and fifty.' He shook his head from side to side inhaling noisily through clenched teeth. 'I'll say this about myself: I'll never get very far in this TV racket. I'm just far too soft.'

11

Shortly after ten on Tuesday morning John Alex Maclean arrived at the office of Iomhaigh Productions. Duncan Sinclair was speaking softly into the telephone. As Maclean dragged himself over to the settee and took off his jacket and shoes his assistant said, 'Please excuse me – got to go.' He replaced the phone and tidied the papers on his desk. Turning his full attention on his now supine boss he said, 'You look knackered, John Alex. What kept you in Ireland all this time?'

'Oh, we came back last Friday,' Maclean said. 'I've been staying at Donna's gaff.' He paused for a few seconds. 'She'll be the death of me, that girl.'

'Filthy job,' Sinclair said, 'but somebody's got to do it. Isn't that how it goes?'

'Beyond filth, Duncan,' Maclean said. 'That girl has positively no shame. I got warning of that on the flight over there. No sooner were the seat belts fastened than she started quizzing me about the chances of her getting work in the television industry. I tried to give her some avuncular advice. "Well, Donna, you're still awfully young, and you'd increase your chances if you went to university first," I said.

' "Why," she says, "would I do that?" Well, she might be young but she's cunning. So cunning was she that she

89

left the top three buttons of her blouse open, and maybe that's what got me all confused. "You'll learn . . . you know . . . like . . . er, stuff," I stammered. "You'll get to meet people . . . you know . . . like . . . men." Believe me, this is no rookie we're talking about here. I almost fainted when she whispered, "I've met plenty of people. It's not difficult for me to meet men. And I've nothing to learn about pleasuring the men I do meet." And she was telling the truth.'

Sinclair gave a yelp of laughter. 'You didn't get to see much of the festival, then?'

'We saw enough,' Maclean said, 'but that's not the reason I went there in the first place. I didn't go to watch films. I went to see people. I wanted to establish contacts with the Irish, the Welsh and the Bretons. In particular, the Spanish. The Galicians are the ones who're really progressive. I didn't take to the Welsh at all, at all, at all. They're not like us. No, they're so mean. My own granny knew that. My grandfather was "on the beach", as they used to say, one time in South Wales when he was going to sea. The landlady of the house where he was staying in Cardiff was so mean she wasn't giving him food at all. My grandmother had to send relief food parcels from Lighthill in Back all the way to Wales to prevent him dying of starvation while he waited for a berth on a ship down there. Oh, I wasn't shy about telling them in *Yr Iaith Gymraeg* about their parsimony. I'm sure I made some enemies among the Taffies when I was over there.'

'You've made an enemy here, too.'

'Who?'

'Kerr,' Sinclair said.

'Catch me if I swoon,' Maclean said. 'I don't give a fig – I think that's the word I'm looking for.'

'He was in here last Thursday,' Sinclair said, 'bragging about how he'd prised a thousand pounds out of Campbell. And he's been phoning every day since then wanting to speak to you.'

'Good for old Donald Campbell,' Maclean said. 'He must have found some kind of banker. The kind of guy Donald is, according to what I hear about him, he's never seen a thousand pounds in one place in his entire life. But with regards to Kerr: forget him. I'll put him in his place.'

'But, John Alex,' Sinclair said, 'we'd better keep in with Kerr. He's on the board at North, isn't he?'

'What if he is?' Maclean said, holding his head in both hands. 'Come here a minute. Have you such a thing as aspirin in here? I'm in excruciating pain – a pain that's wracking my poor body ceaselessly.'

'Where's the pain?'

'In North Television. I think it's a new virulent disease I've contracted. George's Syndrome – that's what it's called.'

'I've had a wee bout of that myself while you and Donna were away.'

'I'm sure you have,' Maclean said. 'I'm also sure you handle it better than I do. You're ten years younger than me, Duncan, and, as I've frequently observed, young people have greater reserves of stamina. Young Donna proved that.'

'Forget about Donna if you can, John Alex. The road

91

ahead is pretty slippery. We've got to keep in Kerr's good books. He still has influence in North. Why don't you try and get on with him, man? He's not here all the time anyway. He went home to Perth last weekend. Said he wouldn't be back in Glasgow until next week.'

'Why is he coming here next week?'

'I'd say he wants, you know, to keep an eye on things,' Sinclair said. 'He's the executive producer of the series, mind. Or he's just missing the outstanding beauty of this place.' He looked round the office and gave a deep sigh. 'Do you know this, John Alex? This place is an absolute tip.'

'I know,' Maclean said. 'Our office needs a makeover, give it a bit of class. We've got to look the part. I'll bring Donna in as receptionist. She'll be hopeless at the IT, but she can answer the phone and she has . . . well, other good points. We'll put prints on the wall – a splash of Monet perhaps – and there's that guy from North Uist, and we can tart the place up with a state-of-the-art sound system . . . Stuff like that.' He paraded round the room in his stocking soles, greatly enthused. 'I'll tell you what you'll do, Duncan. Take a notebook and pen with you and nip up to the ITR offices up in Park Circus. You know, the mob who're responsible for siphoning the millions of pounds off our friends in the STG? Say to Linda, that's Ben Traynor's assistant, say to her that you work for me – no, you work *with* me – at Iomhaigh Productions and that we're going to fix this slum up and that you want to borrow some furnishing ideas from them that we could use down here in sunny Partick. They'll be made up with the flattery, and you can kid on you're taking note of all the prints they have on their walls, what kind of sound and vision systems they have – stuff like that, know what I mean?'

'Sure,' Duncan Sinclair said drily. 'All I have to do is crash in there like Scarface and say: "Hi, Linda and Ben, I'm with Iomhaigh. My boss has fallen in love with your office décor, so I hope you don't mind if I take an inventory of every piece of furniture you've got under your roof, all right?" Leave it out, John Alex. You're making a clown out of me, man.'

'You've never really appreciated my knowledge and experience, Duncan,' Maclean said. 'I know Bob Traynor at the ITR, and plenty of other folk, too. Before I retired from my post at the university – more accurately, when I first heard of the proposed injection of millions of pounds into Gaelic broadcasting – I worked really hard at making the acquaintance of every soul who had been, was and is still working in provincial broadcasting. I recognised very early on that if I were to be successful in this business I'd have to get to know everybody in the racket. You see, dear boy, television, even Gaelic television, is no different from any other business. Good contacts beat ability every time. Of course, if there's an able person out there whom I want, I hire him or her – as I did with your good self, Duncan. They're all my personal friends, these movers and shakers. Bob Traynor at the Independent Television Registry, Gordon Anderson at North Television, Angus Mackenzie and Flora Macdonald at the STG, I've made it my business to ingratiate myself with the lot. I'm in with them all, and that's the most important thing.'

93

'You've been forced in with George Kerr,' Sinclair said. 'Would you call him a close personal friend?'

Maclean shook his head rapidly from side to side. 'Kerr? That was a mistake – that shouldn't have happened. I didn't want him from the very beginning. I told Anderson that time and time again. You see, when I formed Iomhaigh, it was to North I went with my plans and projections. And North proved very good to me. They certainly were that . . .'

'May I ask in what way they were good to you?'

'You may, but I'm not going to tell you everything. When I approached them the year before last, their eye-teeth were hurting to be associated with an independent production company – you know, of course, there's only a handful of specialist Gaelic production companies worthy of the name, and they're all tied to Albion – so, when I popped up, North Television courted me vigorously, you better believe it. They're the ones who funded me so I could rent this henhouse we're in at present. In addition, they gave me money to buy editing equipment and to hire someone who knew a bit about making television programmes. That's you, Duncan. Take a bow. On top of that they commissioned me to make programmes, rubbishy trash initially, which they would broadcast. This was a commission worth a quarter of a million over three years. Not bad, but not all that good either. And . . . they placed an unbearable restraint on me.'

'George Kerr.'

'You've got it in one,' Maclean said. 'To make a long story boring, the board of North Television in Perth have no work for George Kerr. Him a producer? He can't even produce a son and heir. If it wasn't for that ugly woman he's married to, he'd still be using last year's diary. The man's idle up there, and Anderson thought he'd get shot of him by firing him down here, to annoy me and get under my feet. We'll have to do something.'

'If I understand you properly,' Sinclair said, 'what you're saying is: Kerr doesn't have any power up at North, right?'

'He hasn't,' Maclean said. 'And I'm telling you: after all the effort I've put into forming Iomhaigh Productions, I'm not going to let a rude little twerp like Kerr handicap either me or the company.'

'I can't see what can be done, John Alex.'

'Gaelic Television Council.'

'*Sgioba Telebhisean Gàidhlig* – the STG?'

'The very ones,' Maclean said. 'It's the STG that holds the key to this . . . er, locked door. I'll arrange a meeting with them, no expense spared in the hospitality stakes, for, say, next Monday or Tuesday. And when I've softened them up, I'll make a formal complaint against Kerr.'

'Well, as you're well aware, John Alex,' Sinclair said, 'I know nothing about the politics here. What I like to do is make programmes. I'm just grateful you gave me the chance to do that.'

'So you should be, my boy,' Maclean said, 'and don't you ever forget it. When I think back on your appointment, maybe I was lucky when I took a chance on the drunken Barraman. I'm sure plenty of folk had plenty to say when I gave you the job. "Watch it, John Alex," they surely said. "You're offering a job to a young man who read law at the university – a bare Ordinary BL – who got a job at the Beeb and subsequently got the bullet? A guy who admits to having issues with alcohol abuse and who's still only twenty-seven? This fellow's a three-legged pup and he'll never be able to run. You hire a guy with that kind of history, and you're going to let him run your business?" If I'd been thinking like that, Duncan, before I took you on, I'd never have given you the job.'

'I've told you already,' Sinclair said. 'I'm deeply grateful. What do you want from me? Okay, I'm a leper in Highland circles. You want an arm?' He made a squeaking noise in his throat as he mimed screwing off an arm. 'There you go. Have an arm, John Alex.'

Maclean guffawed uninhibitedly. 'That's funny, Duncan. A lawyer with a sense of humour! Who'd have thought it?' He paused with his forefinger raised to his nose as though he had just thought of something. 'Listen, do you know this Ciarán MacRitchie fellow on the committee of the STG?'

'Should I?'

'Well, he's about the same age as you, studied law at Glasgow, a deracinated cove from Stornoway. No Gaelic of course. Despises Maus like us. Have you come across him?'

'Don't think so,' Sinclair said.

'Strikes me as a bit of a geek,' Maclean said. 'Though I detest these *ad hominem* arguments, this man wears a beret. Does a bit of scribbling and loves meeting fellow gays at literary workshops and festivals. Doesn't ring a bell?'

'No, John Alex,' Sinclair said. 'And I'm not interested in guys whose names are obviously Schneider. "Ciarán" – Fenian Paddy – and "MacRitchie" – stone Teuchter Hun. Guy with a name like that can't be the clean potato. The only name that interests me today is Kerr. What are you going to do about George Kerr?'

'Kerr is a dyed-in-the wool crosspatch, and I can't be patient for much longer. He'll have to be replaced.'

'Where is all this rebellious talk going to leave us?'

'In the offices of the Independent Television Registry. That's where you'll be left, Duncan. For me, I think I'd better have a little spell of R&R at Donna's before the battle commences between me – sorry, between us, Duncan – and George Kerr.'

'What do you mean "us"?' Sinclair said. 'You're not big enough to take on the likes of Kerr.'

'I'm going to destroy him,' Maclean said. 'And the sooner the better.' He put his jacket and shoes back on and marched towards the door. He turned towards Sinclair and spoke: 'Fear is worse than actual war.'

12

The bar in the Hilton Hotel in Glasgow was comparatively quiet in the early evening, with a handful of middle-aged well-dressed men sitting on their own at glass-topped tables reading or writing on laptops while taking sips from the glasses of wine and spirits in front of them.

Ciarán MacRitchie, twenty-nine years of age, doffed his beret with a flourish to reveal blond highlights in long light brown hair, as he stood in the entrance scanning the room. When he recognised his boss, Angus John Mackenzie, director of the STG, and vice-chair of the same quango, Flora Macdonald, sitting alongside a tall, thin man in an Armani suit, he drifted slowly towards them. The thin man, obviously the one they called the Prof extended his right hand. MacRitchie hesitated for a couple of seconds as though unsure of what the other man wanted. He instantly identified the man as a breeder just as soon as he enveloped Maclean's hand in his weak grip. 'Doctor Maclean,' he said, 'it's indeed an honour to meet you. Angus John? Flora? Sorry I'm late. What'll you all have?'

'I'll take a nip,' Mackenzie said, a red-faced man in his fifties with the complexion of a careless beekeeper, who had been a primary school head teacher before his elevation to the post of director. 'No. Get me a double, Ciarán.'

'I don't want anything,' Flora Macdonald said. 'I've still got a lot to do tonight. Are we going to eat right away?'

'We can,' Maclean said, as he handed his glass to MacRitchie. 'I'll have a glass of house red, Ciarán, please.' He kept his eyes on MacRitchie as the treasurer of the STG strolled over to the bar counter. 'I thought,' he said, 'I might give you a brief account of how we're getting on with *Cuid do Chroinn* first of all, before we order.'

'On you go, then,' Mackenzie said. 'But get a move on. We have a meeting – Flora and I – down in London tomorrow at Centre One. Have you finished my keynote address yet, Flora?'

'I'm still working on it,' Flora Macdonald said, gritting her teeth.

'Good for you, pet,' Mackenzie said. He craned his neck to get a better view of the bar. 'I wonder what's keeping Ciarán with the drams? Okay, John Alex, what've you got to tell us about *Cuid do Chroinn*. Nothing wrong, I hope?'

'No, no,' Maclean said. 'Well . . .' He stopped. 'That's not entirely true. Iomhaigh Productions have a sterling work in the pre-production stage. We are ensuring that we have a great programme and that there will be no snags when we go into the studio in three weeks' time. But I am a tad concerned.'

'Is it Sinclair you're worried about?' Mackenzie said. 'He drinks too much, that one . . . I mean, for a young lad.'

'Oh, there's nothing much wrong with Sinclair,' Maclean said. 'I've got him on a short leash, you know, spending a lot of time training him up for the job, and I think he'll get there yet.'

'That's good,' Mackenzie said. 'You've got to deal with those young ones with a firm hand, you know.'

'Campbell,' Flora Macdonald said. Both the men looked wide-mouthed at her astonishing interruption. After a brief pause she continued: 'Donald Campbell's the bold boy who's getting up your nose, isn't he?'

'Not at all,' Maclean said. 'I fully expect Donald Campbell to be exceptionally good in the role of presenter. That is . . . you know . . . if he's allowed to do *Cuid do Chroinn*.' Maclean stopped talking for a whole beat. 'Oh, don't worry, he'll certainly do the programme. The trouble is, he's got a problem with an outstanding debt just now – well, that's what they're telling me anyway. But I'll work something out with him, and when I do, he'll be awesome as front man for *Cuid do Chroinn*. I haven't the slightest doubt about that.'

'Lucky you,' Mackenzie said, as he stretched out his hand for the double whisky MacRitchie had placed on the table in front of him. 'I need this! I know what kept you, Ciarán. I was watching you flirting with that tall blond waiter behind the counter. Gave him your telephone number, didn't you? And you drank a couple of extra glasses over there, too.' He gulped down a large mouthful of spirits and gave a lip-smacking gasp of satisfaction. 'Better watch it, lad, before you get too fond of the hard stuff.'

'He's not the only one turning into a jakie,' Flora Macdonald said.

MacRitchie sat on the arm of the settee and looked down on Maclean. He favoured the older man with his most fetching boyish smile. 'Why are we here anyway, Doctor Maclean?'

'That's a good question,' Maclean said. 'The long and the short of it is: I have a complaint.' He inhaled noisily before resuming. 'I'm being compromised by George Kerr.'

'How?' Mackenzie said. 'I know he's a wee bit old-fashioned in his ways, but you've got to remember, John Alex, he's been in the business for nearly thirty years.'

'I sometimes think he's been that time on my back,' Maclean said. 'He's as tight as a First Bus window, always obsessing about money. George Kerr is suffocating me. I am unable to endure the situation any longer. We simply must get another executive producer for *Cuid do Chroinn*.'

'I don't know what advice to give you, John Alex,' Mackenzie said. 'What do you think, Ciarán?'

Ciarán MacRitchie brought both his hands, fingertips touching, up to his chin and addressed Maclean in a deep, rich baritone voice. 'You, Doctor Maclean, and he had a disagreement, right? The question is: is this mutual antipathy going to affect the series?'

'Without a shadow of a doubt,' Maclean said.

'Well,' MacRitchie said confidently, 'if that is the case, I think you should ask North Television to appoint another executive producer. Anderson'll wear that, surely. You and he are pretty close, I hear. But, of course, it's the programmes that make up the paramount consideration.'

'Oh, definitely, definitely,' Mackenzie said. 'The pro-grammes have to be good – that's what we all want.' He raised his empty glass. 'Who's for another?'

'None of you needs another,' Flora Macdonald said angrily. 'What you need are brains. Every one of you. It's not within your power, John Alex, as producer of *Cuid do Chroinn*, to give the executive producer his P45. What Iomhaigh have to do is create the programmes. What North have to do is broadcast those programmes. They've got to ensure they're of broadcast standard and, so, they appoint someone to supervise the project. They've done that. It just so happens they've appointed George Kerr to that position. That's your tough luck, John Alex, but it was never inscribed on the tablets of Moses that you'd get your own way every time. Buy him some flowers and chocolates, and the next time you see him ask him if he'll catch you if you swoon before the shining example of his exquisite career. And, moreover, John Alex, I don't consider it our task to offer advice on a subject like this. Our duty is to service the funding and to introduce independent production companies to broadcasters. That's all. We've no business interfering in inter-company policies.' She removed her document case from her lap and stood up. 'If we have nothing else to discuss, I'm going up to my room. I'll maybe get a bite to eat before I finish off your speech, Angus John.'

'Hold on, Flora,' Maclean said. 'Won't you admit he's not one of our own people? He has a smattering of Gaelic right enough, but he'll never ever come close to our true feelings. Wouldn't it be better to get a Gael for the job? What about Carol Macleod at Albion? Or surely there's some suitable person at the Beeb.'

'Light of my life,' Flora Macdonald said, 'watch my

lips. Carol Macleod does not work for North. She is a highly paid employee of Albion Television. Anyway, you'd regret it bitterly if Carol the Terminator landed in your lap.'

'Just a moment, Ms Macdonald,' Ciarán MacRitchie said, 'I don't see anything wrong with Albion providing an executive for North – as a one-off. They work in an environment of mutual aid, don't they?'

'Yeah, and there's a squadron of pigs flying outside the window as we speak,' Flora Macdonald said.

'I maintain that Carol is eminently capable. I know this to my own cost. She was Dux of the Nicolson Institute in my sixth year there.'

'Well, the pair of you certainly went to a good school, unlike some of us who had to attend academies in Fort William and Dumfries,' Flora Macdonald said. 'I don't know if you remember, Ciarán, but when her ladyship was just a schoolgirl she knew more about fleecing folk for money than they did in the Kasbah in Tangiers.'

'Now that you mention it,' MacRitchie said, 'I seem to remember her telling me after she graduated in accountancy she was going in for something called hedge fund management. Wonder what made her change her mind.'

'Hormones,' Flora Macdonald said. 'That and a well-heeled smoothy called Gus Miller.'

'If I can break up this blistering Socratic dialogue,' Mackenzie said, taking a mouthful of whisky from his glass, 'I'd just like to say that John Alex has a valid point here. George is certainly not one of us. He is what we call at home a grey squirrel.'

'It seems to me,' Flora Macdonald said, 'that I'm not one of you either. Thank goodness. Are you all so sozzled by drink you don't understand what I'm saying? North Television is the nominated broadcaster. They picked George Kerr as the executive producer. That's all, she wrote. Get over it.'

Emboldened by the presence of the tall, blond waiter at a table nearby, Ciarán MacRitchie raised his voice in protest. 'I beg to disagree with you, Ms Macdonald,' he said. 'As you know, I studied law at university, something that none of you ever did, and my opinion is that Kerr should be relieved of his duties forthwith. Removing him and appointing someone else shouldn't be all that difficult.' He beckoned the blond waiter and held up four fingers. He intoned his summation in a loud voice: 'I know this much: if I were in John Alex's shoes and if somebody, anybody, was placing a project of mine in danger because of parsimony, I'd have no hesitation in getting rid of him . . . or her.'

Mackenzie drained his glass and turned his gaze on Maclean. 'Do you see, John Alex, what a merciless terrier I have as one of my disc— one of my valued team? He's always threatening me. Now what bully is going to force me into having another dram?'

'What do you want, Angus John?' Maclean said. He ordered two whiskies and a glass of wine from the handsome youth who was standing very close to MacRitchie. 'Angus John,' he said, 'all I want is your permission to go to Anderson and ask him to appoint a different executive producer. I wouldn't make a move without getting clearance from you, know what I mean?'

'Go ahead,' MacRitchie said. 'Give him the elbow. Life's too short to be pussyfooting around. Is that us finished now? I'd like to get out of this place. It's so dead.'

'Funny that,' Maclean said, 'I've organised something for later on that may appeal to you. That is, if you fancy a bite of Middle Eastern food and a few drams in an interesting little ethnic place I've discovered on St George's Road . . . Angus John, what should I do?'

'Just do as you think fit,' Mackenzie said. 'Tell us more about this intriguing place you've got lined up for us.'

'Well, I thought we'd go . . .' He stopped in mid-sentence. 'It seems that Flora may be too busy and not want to accompany us to the house of the Turkish belly dancer. Accordingly, I thought you two might enjoy a visit to Bosphorus to eat first of all – a really amazing little hardbody the dancer they have performing there – and that we'd then go on to the Ben Lomond or someplace like it for a few drams.' He took a deep breath before continuing. 'And then, perhaps, we could take a trip over to the South side to a place a pal of mine owns, Desert Palms – we can have a body massage there – and, who knows, maybe we'll go back to my flat for . . . Well, we'll see what happens, know what I mean?'

'That'd be very good,' Mackenzie said.

'Rain check,' MacRitchie said as he looked anxiously towards the bar where the waiter was tapping his watch with a forefinger.

Flora Macdonald took her napkin from her lap and let it fall on to the table. 'Well,' she said, 'excuse me, gentlemen. Some of us have work to do. And if you want my advice,

John Alex, keep clear of George Kerr. Irrespective of what my two colleagues say, we don't have enough power, as Gaels, to take on the Lowlanders who're deeply entrenched in television. Not yet anyway.' She got to her feet. 'Don't get up, gentlemen. Avoid confrontation with Kerr, Doctor Maclean. In the eyes of the grey squirrels you're no bigger than a dot. And that truly is tiny.' She bared her teeth and gave a mocking laugh. 'But the girls in Desert Palms will no doubt tell you that later on tonight.'

13

At half past ten in the morning of the seventh of March, outside the Central Railway Station in Glasgow, a row of black cabs waited in line for travellers. At high speed MacAskill turned his yellow Volkswagen Caravelle right from Renfield Street into Gordon Street and stopped alongside the leading taxi in the queue. From the rear of the van Campbell said, 'There she is, Calum Iain. Over there – at the station entrance.'

Mary MacLennan, a statuesque woman with long black hair, around twenty-seven years of age, crouched down on one knee when she heard MacAskill sounding his horn. She lifted a bulky suitcase easily and walked with some poise on six-inch high heels over to the Caravelle.

MacAskill leaned over and opened the passenger door. Mary ducked inside, placing the case neatly on her lap. 'Right, Donald,' she said, 'grab hold of the case and sling it anywhere in the back.' She passed the suitcase back to Campbell and kissed MacAskill lightly on the cheek. 'You smell nice, Calum Iain,' she said. 'What is it?'

'Thank you, Mary,' MacAskill said. 'It's Lacoste. It's pretty expensive.'

'He's telling porkies, Mary,' Campbell's voice came from behind. 'This is new stuff that comes from the old spectacle factory in Barra. *Rùda*, it's called. Ram.

Has a fearful effect on the females. The first time I tried it myself was at a gig in the Whalers' Rest in Stornoway. In the audience that night were a group of fat ladies from the Harris WeightWatchers, two bus loads of Shearings pensioners and' – he coughed – 'a dozen ewes from Alex Fat's "lot" in the *Gleann Dubh*. Oh, I'm telling you, that Ram is powerful stuff, without a doubt.'

'Must have been too much of it – power, I mean – around that night in the gym at Balivanich,' Mary MacLennan said. 'Do you remember, Donald, that ram from Gerinish who came onto me with an offer of a black-and-white Hereford bull calf and a second-hand Land-Rover if I'd go back to the croft with him?'

'Was that the night of the big fight at the concert?' Campbell said.

'There was a fight at a concert?' MacAskill said.

'No, that's not the night I'm talking about,' Mary said. 'I was in the audience the night of the big fight at the concert. That was in Eochar Hall. I was still a pupil in Daliburgh School then. No, this was a dance in Benbecula a couple of years later and you had me on the bill. That was the first time I did an island tour with you, Donald. Do you not remember the night the tribe of Finlay from the Middle District paid us a visit?'

'Oh, yes indeed,' Campbell said, 'I remember that night very well.'

'Did another fight take place that night?' MacAskill said.

'No,' Mary MacLennan said, 'it was just the usual high jinks that take place at island gatherings – sex, strong drink and, instead of rock'n'roll, cattle.'

Campbell released a merry yelp of laughter. 'That's right, Mary. It's true that descendant of old Finlay didn't want to let you return to your mother in the same condition you were in when you arrived. Black designs he had on you that night. Word filtered down to the committee room that something bizarre was going to happen at the dance.' He prodded MacAskill's left arm. 'Make a left at the next turn-off, Calum Iain. Go on for about half a mile and you'll come to a slip-road that'll take us onto the motorway.'

MacAskill turned into Cowcaddens. 'What did you hear?' he said. 'What horrible event was about to take place? Who told you about it?'

'The lads on the committee told us,' Campbell said, 'that they'd heard – and Willie MacEachan's face was a ghastly shade of grey and a gross tremor overcame his body . . .'

'What?' MacAskill said.

'That the sons of Finlay were on their way to the dance,' Mary MacLennan said.

'And that's exactly what happened,' Campbell said, 'at two o'clock in the morning, on the dot. And the red-headed hooligan – was his name Ronald? – was at the head of a team of about ten hooligans who marched up to the stage looking for a fight. He scowled at the dancers who stood below, gazing fearfully upwards. The bold Ronald looked around the silenced crowd and saw that his world was good. The next thing was, he saw Mary here standing demurely at the door of the committee room and he assumed the posture of a poacher who spots a twelve-pointer stag on Eabhal.

111

'His neck seemed to scrunch down into his shoulders, and his eyes narrowed while his mouth gaped in astonishment. He stretched his arms out on either side of his coiled body like some old preacher. He transferred his gaze to the dancers below. His face contorted into a rictus of agony. "Ladies and gentlemen," he brayed, "you all know who it is who's addressing you tonight. I am Ronald, son of Finlay, son of red-headed John, son of Michael. Hear my tribute. Even though I were to spend the next thousand years coming down from Gerinish to Benbecula in order to attend dances at the gym, I should never see between my two eyes a maid as beautiful as the tall dark girl from North Uist I can see standing by the committee room door this very moment. Here are my proposals, and they are as fresh as though delivered five minutes ago on the slopes of Mount Sinai: If She Will Sleep With Me Tonight I Will Give Her A Second-Hand Land-Rover Worth Eight Hundred Pounds. And A Black-And-White Hereford Bull Calf." '

'Cringe, cringe,' MacAskill said. 'What did you do, Donald?'

'Well, I walked right up to him,' Campbell said, 'and I've got to admit my heart was in my mouth. This was one big guy. And he was very drunk. I had absolutely no idea what I was going to do.'

'Don't listen to him, Calum Iain,' Mary MacLennan said. 'He was magnificent. The monster says: "Hey, you know what, that girl of yours is very attractive. How would you feel about lending her to me for the night?" Campbell here is as cool as a mountain stream. "Quite bad, actually,"

112

he says. "Well, how about if I just ignored you," my horny suitor says, "and simply threw her over my shoulder and left?" "I don't know about that," says my hero, Mr Campbell. "How about you leaving and letting us get on with the dance?"'

'Frankenstein replies: "I'd actually feel pretty bad about that, because I really fancy a night with that girl." My hero looks him in the eye and says: "Is that so? Too bad."

'Bad move. The caveman gives a loud laugh like a horse whinnying. "Ha-ha-ha! Too bad?" Campbell keeps his cool. "That's right. Listen, I'm sorry to disappoint you, but the lady's not going anywhere, especially not to Gerinish." The freak from Gerinish is laughing but he's not very happy. "Ha-ha-ha. Who's going to stop me from doing what I like?"

'This was Campbell's finest hour. "You obviously feel that you have to behave like a bully," he says. "Now I'm going to behave like a bully, too." Lover boy bunches his fists and says in sneering tones: "Are you telling me you'd be able to stop me?"

' "Here's your money back," Mr Campbell here says, and he allows a pound note to flutter to the floor. "You need to leave right now." Surprisingly, my bridegroom-to-be takes this like a traffic accident. "Okay," he says, "so I'll just have to wait outside for you, I suppose." My protector, Mr Donald Campbell, bachelor of this parish, doesn't bat an eyelid. "That's fine," he says. "See you at the close of Sunday School."

'We watched the gang filing out the hall to the accompaniment of slow hand-clapping from the dancers,' Mary MacLennan said. 'It was a magic moment.' She paused for a beat and smiled at Campbell. 'I guess, Donald, you owe me a second-hand Land-Rover, though.'

'And a black-and-white Hereford bull calf,' said Campbell.

'Were they outside waiting for you when the dance finished?' MacAskill said.

'Naw,' Campbell said. 'Either they tanned the carry-out they had and forgot about us, or he bumped into an extraordinarily skilled psychotherapist in the car park who counselled him successfully. I don't know, and I don't care. Just another example of weirdness.'

'That was a narrow escape you guys had,' MacAskill said. 'Good job there won't be anything like that up in Fort William tonight . . . Will there?'

'No, I'm sure there won't,' Mary MacLennan said. 'The only thing I'd be a bit windy about if I were you, Calum Iain, would be the naughty girls of Caol. Particularly with the smell of Lacoste you're giving off there.'

'What are you getting at?' MacAskill said. 'Who are the naughty girls of Caol?'

'Will you tell him about them, Donald?' Mary MacLennan said.

'What have you got to tell me?' MacAskill said.

'Listen carefully to me, Calum Iain,' Campbell said. 'When we wrap tonight, you'll be going for a pint, won't you?'

'Aye,' MacAskill said, 'there's a good chance I will.'

'Well, there's a good chance that some lust-crazed

114

groupie will come up to you and ask you if you want to go to a party, am I right?'

'So what?' MacAskill said.

'Oh, it's nothing to me,' Campbell said. 'Just as long as you're back at the Centre at three o'clock. We're heading back at three, remember. But if you get an invitation, or you're on a promise, tonight, I don't care how beautiful she is, or how drunk she is – we all know you'd prefer a girl who's gorgeous and smart, but you'll take an ugly one who's blind drunk any time – if a girl asks you to go along with her to a party, will you promise me you'll do one particular thing before you accept?'

'What do you want me to do?' MacAskill said.

'Ask her where she comes from,' Campbell said. 'If she says Kilmallie Road take to your heels immediately. If she's from Achintore, that's all right. See her home and enjoy a mug of Horlicks with her. That's allowed. But if it's one of these girls from Caol, avoid her like the . . .'

'Like a dose of the crabs?' Mary MacLennan said.

'Just don't get involved with one of them,' Campbell said. 'They're really tough when they're in heat.'

There was silence within the van for a full five seconds. MacAskill suddenly turned his head to his left and posed a tentative question. 'What do you mean "tough"?'

'This is the honest truth,' Campbell said. 'The last time I went home with one of them, she gave me the fright of my life. Before we even went into the bedroom she put a sweatband round her forehead and she handed me a crash-helmet, and she said: "It's just for your own protection, darlin'. Things could get really rough in here tonight, know what I mean?" They're too rich for my blood, man.'

'And they certainly know what they want,' Mary Mac-Lennan said chuckling, 'once they get you into bed, don't they, Donald?'

'Oh, they're not shy at all,' Campbell said, 'not a bit of it. You're not allowed to go to sleep afterwards. You know, as you usually do, when you've satisfied yourself, you turn your back on them, and in a heartbeat or two you're drifting off to sleep. Well, that's no longer allowed nowadays. As soon as you've finished hammering a job for her, that's it. *Demino*. They want shot of you right away. They poke you and shout "Hey! Hey! Hey! Get out of my bed! Both of you! You and your pal! Out! Out!"'

'I don't understand, Donald,' MacAskill said. 'What does she mean "You and your pal, both of you?" I can't see . . .'

'Don't look, then,' Mary MacLennan said. 'That was just one of the routines Donald uses in his act. Are you going to use the whole thing tonight, Donald?'

'I don't know,' Campbell said. 'When I go out in front of people, I don't even have a plan in my head. Well, I know how I'm going to start my routine, and I make damn sure I know exactly how I'm going to finish up, but in between, I just throw the cards I have in my head up in the air and I try to grab as many of them as I can as they come down. And I pray that the audience are following all the twists and turns I make in the overall narrative. You know yourself how important that is, Calum Iain. But of course we're different, you and I. You'd better arrange a running order for Mary's songs – and your own sets, too, Calum

116

Iain. Can I borrow your heavy coat, Mary? I think I'll have a wee zizz in the back here. Give me a shake when we arrive at Fort William.'

'Well, Donald,' MacAskill said, 'I don't believe you're as relaxed as you make out. Are you not nervous about the show tonight?'

'No reason to be,' Campbell said. 'Tonight, and every other night, too, there are only two things worth worrying about – yourself and the audience. You'll either be good or you'll be rotten. Most of the time, I think, you'll be middling. When it comes to audiences, that's a different matter altogether. Maybe you'll have a good crowd in. Perhaps hardly anyone'll turn up. If we get a packer tonight, it doesn't really matter if you're good or bad. You take the money and run. You'll probably not get a return invitation if you put up an indifferent show, but you will get paid. With a poor turn-out you're in trouble. You can moon in front of them, take your kidneys out for them and melt into a wee greasy spot at the end of the night, all for the sake of a scabby pound or two. And the paradox is: you'd better pull out all the stops when you're performing in front of a small audience because, if you're half decent and the majority like you, at best you just might get an invitation to come back.'

Campbell lay back on the bench seat in the back of the van and wrapped himself in Mary MacLennan's heavy coat. 'Here endeth the lesson, children. I'm only going to say this: don't worry about how you do tonight. You're both very good. Just pray that the Camus Centre will be stowed out tonight. If it is,' and here his voice assumed the

117

oily forced enthusiasm of some shill for scrap gold, 'if we score, the numerous worries of Donald Campbell will disappear like morning dew on the meadow in the heat of the sun.'

'Amen,' Mary MacLennan said.

14

Samuel Johnson knocked on the dressing-room door. He listened to MacAskill and Mary MacLennan chatting together at the bottom of the spiral staircase that led to the stage and the back door of the theatre but could not make out the details of their conversation. The corridor where he was standing was busy with the television folk carrying equipment outside to their vans in the car park beyond the stage door. He listened with his ear pressed against the door with the star in tinsel attached to it, but no sound came from inside. He tried the handle. The door was unlocked. He entered the dimly lit room. Only one bulb shone in the horseshoe of lights surrounding the dressing-table mirror. In the middle of the carpet Campbell lay on his back, unconscious. There were three large whisky bottles, almost empty, standing upright, and several cans of beer, on a shelf that ran below a row of mirrors on one of the walls.

The deputy manager of the Camus Centre placed his leather bag on the floor beside Campbell's head. He lifted one of the cans, opened it and sat down on the swivel chair. He spoke softly, gently: 'Mr Campbell? Are you okay, Mr Campbell?'

Campbell came awake immediately and suddenly sat up. He lit a Marlboro and as soon as he took his first puff he was racked by a heavy cough. His face was red and there were tears in his eyes. 'Who're you?' he said between gasps.

Johnson lifted another can from the shelf and extended it to Campbell.

'What on earth are you doing here?' Campbell said. 'What's going on?'

'Hair of the dog,' Johnson said with a conspiratorial smile. 'I'm Sam Johnson, deputy manager of this place. We've got to talk. You fit?'

'You proposing marriage?' Campbell said as he rose and moved over to the sink. He proceeded to empty the beer into the sink and, when done, he carelessly tossed the empty can into the wastebasket. 'If you're after my hand in marriage, or indeed any other part of my anatomy, I'm obliged to tell you I'm actively pursued by widows in three counties and you've no need to ply me with booze. I'm off it – just now, anyway. Let's just talk about money, Mr Johnson.'

'I thought . . .' Johnson said. 'I thought . . . I was under the impression . . .'

'I was rubbered?' Campbell said. 'Sorry to disappoint you, Sam. Just doing my relaxation exercises. Little tip I picked up in the last puzzle factory I was in. You know, a spin-dryer? Detox facility? Never mind, what's on your mind?'

'I'm so sorry!' Johnson said. 'Abasements and apologies, Mr Campbell.'

'Easy mistake to make,' Campbell said. 'You see the empty booze bottles lying around – hospitality for honoured guests and assorted freeloaders, but you didn't know that. You clock a guy who's described as a walking syringe flaked out on the deck, and you put two and two together and . . .'

'Got five,' Johnson said with a grin. 'I'm sorry – hey, I'm actually quite glad. I mean . . . Listen, Don, that was some show you put on tonight. I mean, I've only been here for two years, but in that time we've never done better box office. Linda – that's my boss – she's turning cartwheels down in the hospitality suite right now. Probably making plans to bring up another celebrity nobody's ever heard of to do "alternative" comedy or put on a Third World musical ensemble. Never mind that they couldn't fill a phone box. Saying that, the point is pretty straightforward. She gets the chance to be sexually harassed by some brutal ethnic-type person when she goes out to audition acts on location. Anyway, Don, everybody's hyperventilating about your show, and I've got the figures and the cash all ready right here. Fancy going over them with me?'

'You bet I do!' Campbell said.

'Oh, by the way,' Johnson said, 'the horny Linda asked me to deliver this to you.' He brought a brown envelope, rather a fat envelope, out of his bag and handed it to Campbell. 'Is that okay?'

'Is what okay?' Campbell said.

'Look,' Johnson said, 'I'm just the message boy round here. "Take this little token of our appreciation to Mr Campbell immediately, Sam," says the lovely Linda. So I go, "Any message?" and she says, "You might intimate to

Mr Campbell that if he were motivated to pay a return visit to Fort William in the near future, the management here would be inclined to view any application from him to hire the theatre in a favourable light." So I'd say, if you were to ask me, what you've got in your hand is a little present from the lovely Linda. You got any objection to presents?'

'No.'

'Fine,' Johnson said. 'The television guys are over the moon about you, too. How are you making out with this Gaelic television stuff anyway? Got your nose in the feeding trough yet?'

'I think,' Campbell said, 'that things just improved a lot.'

'Gets better,' Johnson said as he handed over another brown envelope that was just as thick as the first one.

'What's this?' Campbell said.

'DVDs and CDs,' Johnson said. 'Minus ten per cent for us, of course. Two hundred and seventy quid for you.' He took a handful of papers from the bag. 'Ready for the numbers?'

Campbell strolled over to the clothes rack and extracted a pen and notebook from the inside pocket of his suit jacket before positioning himself behind Johnson. 'Okay,' he said. 'Go for it.'

'Gross receipts totalled four thousand, five hundred and fifty-three pounds,' Johnson said. 'What we had here was a full house. We got well and truly slammed. That's still not a hundred per cent capacity, mind you. Actually, you can't get a hundred per cent capacity in this house. Eight per cent of the boxes are booked by Phoenix Fabricators – some kind of sponsorship-tax-break deal, I don't know . . .'

'Never mind that,' Campbell said. He wrote in his notebook. 'Your whack?'

'Expenses,' Johnson said, 'for advertising, local radio, newspaper ads, printing.'

'Bottom line,' Campbell said.

'Okay,' Johnson said. 'Bottom line for us comes to one, three, six, oh – a little less than a grand and a half.'

'You guys happy with that, then?' Campbell said. He scribbled some figures into his book.

'Very,' Johnson said. 'The way I get it, it's a fifty-fifty split between you and Albion Television. That means your share comes to just over a grand and a half, right?'

'You got that in cash?' Campbell said as he made further notations in the notebook.

'Sure,' Johnson said. He brought three bundles of notes held together by elastic bands out of his message bag and passed them over to Campbell.

'Thanks,' Campbell said, accepting the cash with one hand and snapping the notebook shut with the other.

'Can I ask you a favour?' Johnson said as he rose to his feet and zipped up his bag.

'Fire away,' Campbell said.

'Could you possibly send me a photograph of Mary MacLennan?' Johnson said. 'And could you get her to sign it "With best wishes to my friend, Sam"?'

'Fancy her, do you?' Campbell said.

'She's gorgeous,' Johnson said. 'I didn't understand what she said – I don't have the Gaelic, you know – but

123

she's got a great voice and she looks terrific. I'll bet she'll have a great future in television. Will you send me her photo?'

'No problem,' Campbell said as he stuffed the money into the pockets of his trousers. 'A guy makes a box-up of the receipts, and I end up in pocket. Man, that's the least I can do.'

'What do you mean a "box-up of the receipts"?'

'Relax, you've still got the job,' Campbell said. 'You see, the deal was that two thirds of the net profits were to go to Albion, one third to me. You gave me half. Don't worry, Sam – they'll probably take the five hundred off my telly fee down the line. But that's later, and it's now we're interested in, right? Theatre's got its money. More importantly, I've got mine.' Campbell sighed deeply and adopted the sonorous tones of a missionary. 'And you'll never know how grateful I am that the lovely Linda went to school on a short bus and didn't bother to check the percentages of Carol Macleod.' He spoke in his normal voice. 'As for the other thing, of course I'll get you Mary's autographed picture. She'll be thrilled you asked for it. I wouldn't bet on our Mary's future success in television though. Let me put this in perspective. Nearly thirty per cent of BBC Scotland's annual programming budget is spent on Gaelic broadcasting – for a little more than one per cent of the population! How long do you think it will be before the heavies down in Glasgow look at the figures and the product and say, "We should really have the nurse pull the screens round this patient, don't you think, Clive?" So, while I agree with you that Mary is talented and not ill to look at, I wouldn't hold my breath for her to make the big break on telly. It's only Gaelic television after all, and in the eyes of our Lowland overlords we're little more than the chunks of rotten mackerel we put in our lobster creels. We're no more than bait, Sam.'

Johnson looked over in the direction of the door and shook his head slowly. 'That's tough. She's, you know, she seems like a lovely person. And you're a nice guy, too, Don.' He grinned broadly as though remembering something that made him happy. 'You're a very funny man . . . and that other guy, he can play a bit, can't he?'

Campbell adopted the Elmer Gantry pose, both arms extended and face raised heavenwards. 'Yes, Sam,' he proclaimed in an adenoidal whine, 'I'm glad I was given the opportunity to be an instrument, if only temporarily, of the Creator's will, and that both of them should have the fangs of the viper removed from their necks. Calum Iain was delivered from crack-cocaine addiction in Kyles Scalpay and poor Mary forsook a life of prostitution on a tidal islet in North Uist. My goodness! If you had seen that sorry pair in the depths of their degradation, you would have run a mile. Mary had her hair full of chewing gum – don't ask, some kind of attempt to sweeten her breath for clients, I suspect – and Calum Iain's nose and mouth were always smothered in glue. Yes, I was privileged to be the instrument of their deliverance. I raised the pair of them out of the gutter, where they both lay, face down, in the stank!'

'Hey, Don,' Johnson said, giggling, 'I just about wet myself at the church elder bit you did tonight. That was great. Oh, and the dentist routine, too – that was hilarious. When'll we get to see them on the telly?'

'I don't know.' Campbell said. 'End of the year some-time.'

'Don?' Johnson said.

'What?'

'You made me really happy tonight,' Johnson said. 'Were you happy?'

'I don't think so,' Campbell said. 'I don't really know what it feels like to be happy.'

'It feels,' Johnson said, 'like tears are coming into your eyes.'

'Oh that,' Campbell said. 'Well then, I suppose I'm happy most of the time.'

15

George Kerr stood inside the doorway of Iomhaigh Productions, mouth agape as he looked round about him. In front of him was an oak desk displaying a slim-line television receiver, laptop, phone and fax machine. A burgundy carpet covered the entire floor. Three watercolours comprising little more than random streaks of primary colours adorned the cream walls. 'Coisich, A Rùin' sung by Capercaillie was belting, at full volume, out of four Bose speakers on gleaming stainless-steel stands placed in each corner of the cramped room.

Donna MacIver, seated behind the desk, stopped applying colour to her nails and smiled broadly at him. Though only around twenty, she gave the impression that she knew stuff. Her hair was raven black and descended in wavy cascades on either side of her heart-shaped face. One diamond-studded earring in her right ear twinkled with much the same pleasing effect that the deep dimples on her cheeks did. Unlike the fair, dry-skinned, pallid progeny of the cloud-swaddled Hebrides, her slender bare arms and her face glowed with shiny copper tones. Above ballet slippers she wore a short Versace skirt and a white sleeveless blouse of Thai silk, cut extremely low in front to show to the world that Donna MacIver was aware of what she had and that she wasn't shy about letting others see it.

'Help you?' she said brightly.

'Doubt it,' Kerr said. 'Gave up playing with skateboards years ago.' He wheeled away and made for the big office on the left.

'Wait,' Donna said, rising to her full five foot ten. 'Doctor Maclean's in conference. Please take a seat and I'll tell him you're here. Who'll I say wants to see him?'

'Sit down, dear,' Kerr said. 'That way you're not a threat.' He coughed. 'Now, listen very carefully. My name's George Kerr. I'm the executive producer of *Cuid do Chroinn*, the series – the sole series, I may add – of Gaelic programmes your testosterone-crazed employer has been commissioned by the STG to produce for my company, North Television. Now, I'm going to go in and see Maclean, and I'm going to do something to him he won't like – oh, I'm not going to hurt him, but he won't be happy about it. While I'm in there, if you can tear yourself away from your new toys, you'll make me a small cup of instant coffee – no milk or sugar – and bring it through. Understood?'

'We've got a new Gaggia,' Donna said. 'I can do you espresso, latte, skinny latte, café solo, café con leche, un cortado . . .'

'Sounds dirty to me,' Kerr said. 'Instant'll do fine. Any questions?'

'Yes, I do have a question,' Donna said. 'What I wanted to ask – you being in television and all – was, well, do you know anything about photocopiers?'

'What?'

'Photocopiers,' Donna said. 'You see, I only started here yesterday and J.A. – I mean, John Alex – he's been kind of

128

busy, and he hasn't had time to show me how to work this machine yet. So, I was, like, wondering . . . I don't want him to think I'm some kind of air-head bimbo, you know? This job's kind of important to me, you know? Every time I press the green button the thing growls at me.' She gave him the sexy face. 'Do you think you could help me, Mr Kerr?'

'Ask Maclean to show you,' Kerr said. 'He's a self-declared expert at pushing people's buttons for them. No doubt you've noticed.' He turned away from her quickly and walked into the small office without even knocking.

Lying on the leather sofa with his legs resting on the desk behind which Sinclair sat in front of a computer was Doctor John Angus Maclean, CEO and founder of Iom-haigh Productions. One bitter word emerged from his mouth: 'Kerr.'

'Got that right, Maclean,' Kerr said. 'Everything else in the gaff you've got terribly wrong.'

'Oh, you've noticed already how things are looking much better around here, have you?'

'I've noticed,' Kerr said, 'that you've turned the office into a brothel. What is that dunderhead doing out there? Don't tell me, John Alex – I know. That's your latest young bit on the side, isn't it?'

'That's Donna,' Maclean said, 'and I'm training her up to be my PA.'

'That's a new word for it,' Kerr said. He turned to Sinclair. 'The pair of you have turned this place into a knocking shop, haven't you? That's the reason for the fitted carpet, the pictures and the music, isn't it?'

'We're just trying to do the place the up,' Sinclair said. 'You know, trying to make us look more . . . er, professional.'

'What does all this cost?' Kerr said.

'Most of the stuff is hired,' Sinclair said. 'The photocopier comes in at around forty-five a month, the pictures cost about twenty, the sound system and the telly are part of a package costing . . . oh, about twenty-five. The carpet and the desk we bought outright. The monthly payments for the other stuff come to around, say, a hundred and sixty. We reckon that people who visit will leave with a good impression of the company.'

'And where will the money for all this come from?' Kerr said. 'Are you going to have Donna selling her body out in the lobby?'

'George,' Maclean said, 'watch your blood pressure. Don't even think about the lovely Donna. It isn't good for your old heart. Every time you mention her name your face goes as red as someone who skipped the midge repellent before going out to the peats. My colleague and I came to the conclusion that it was time to . . . umh, push the boat out. It has nothing to do with you how we spend our money.'

'Have you got the money to spend?' Kerr said. 'I absolutely forbid you to spend a penny of the money allocated to *Cuid do Chroinn* on frippery like this.'

'I have many friends,' Maclean said, 'who are willing to support me financially as long as I provide them with my talent.'

'You'll need them both – friends and talents,' Kerr said.

'I don't think your talents are worth talking about, and when it comes to friends, I know this: you don't have a bigger enemy than me. I am sick and tired of your cavalier attitude. You had no right to put that prime example of jailbait out there on the books without discussing it with me first. You should not have invested in all that flashy tat for the outer office before getting my approval. And you shouldn't have given what you call "development money" to Campbell. Are you aware that he still owes me fifteen hundred pounds? I can do without all these troubles. Have you forgotten that we have a series of programmes to film starting – when, Duncan?'

'A fortnight tomorrow.'

'John Alex,' Kerr said, 'are you going to work with me or against me?'

'Neither.'

'Whatever do you mean?'

'I'm with this guy,' Maclean said waving his hand to indicate Sinclair. 'This is the future of Gaelic television. He has absolutely amazing ideas for programming. And I shan't be slow to put these ideas in front of members of the STG and North Television. People who'll jump at our proposals. Why do we need you?'

'I am the executive director of the only series you've managed to secure so far,' Kerr said.

'You're a suit, George,' Maclean said. 'You're nothing but a suit. When a suit wears out, we get rid of it. And we simply go out and get a new one. I believe I'll be doing that myself soon.'

'Make sure you've a fat wallet in your tail before you go

out,' Kerr said. 'I'm off now, see if I can get hold of Campbell. If I don't get my money off him, I'll put that young man who reads the Gaelic news for us in his place. I leave you with my blessings and I hope you'll all be very happy together – all three of you.' He turned on his heel and almost stumbled into Donna who was carrying a tray with cups and a jug of filtered coffee into the office. 'Oops, young lady,' he said as he swept past her, 'that was a near thing. On second thoughts, ask Sinclair there to show you how to work the photocopier. He's the future of Gaelic television.'

After Kerr's abrupt departure, Maclean and Sinclair remained silent for two minutes. At last, Maclean sighed and said, 'Do you see what I'm talking about, Duncan? We simply have to get rid of that horrible man.'

'He sounded really pissed off.'

'Ah, his bark is worse than his bite,' Maclean said. 'The man's all mouth. Listen to me, he has no real power. I've spoken to the STG about him, and they've given me a green light, or a red and amber at least, to ask North to find somebody else to replace him. I only have to email Anderson – you'll compose it, Duncan – saying that Kerr has become a liability, what with his over-oppressive regime of financial austerity and his inability to get on with the creative staff here at Iomhaigh . . . blah, blah, blah.'

'Shall I mention "irreconcilable artistic differences placing the project in jeopardy"?'

'That's the ticket,' Maclean said. 'I'll ask Donna to send Anderson the email as soon as you've got it finished.' He lifted the phone, pressed one button and spoke softly into the mouthpiece. 'Donna, darling,' he crooned, 'would you come in a minute, please?'

'What're we going to do about Campbell?' Sinclair said.

'Nothing.'

'I know Kerr wasn't kidding when he said he'd get some YTS youth to present the show,' Sinclair said. 'Do you want me to go and try and find Campbell? And get the money, of course?'

'No need,' Maclean said. 'Donald Campbell will present *Cuid do Chroinn*, whatever else happens. Of that I'm sure. Maybe in a week's time Kerr will have disappeared from the frame and nobody will be concerned about the money. If we're required legally to seek restoration we'll just deduct the grand from Donald's wages. Don't let it bother you, Duncan.' He turned his attention on Donna who stood at attention in the doorway, notebook and pen at the ready. 'Donna, light of my life,' he said, employing mellifluous baritone cadences, 'Duncan here is going to write a brief email shortly. He'll save it as a draft on his own laptop, and you'll be able to access it on your machine out there. I want you to email it to Gordon Anderson at North Television. This afternoon, please. When you have done this, you will meet me at Ristorante La Fiorentina in the Merchant City at, say, half past three. I saw a nice strapless dress in Armani next door that'll look breath-taking on you. After purchasing the garment and perhaps some Jimmy Choos to go with it, we shall return here to a quiet and empty office, Duncan having gone home to his plucky little spouse, Anne Marie, in order to recover from

133

earlier exertions, and I personally will instruct you . . . er, in the operation of the various bits of technology in which we have recently invested. Okay?'

Donna looked very concerned. 'J.A., I mean, Doctor Maclean,' she stammered, 'I don't know . . . I feel horribly conflicted.'

' "Conflicted" you say?'

'I'm not sure,' Donna said. 'I'm not very good with inanimate machines, you know. I'm more a kind of hands-on kind of person who prefers dealing with human beings, know what I mean?'

'Mmmm,' Maclean hummed.

'Also, I'm not quite sure,' Donna said, 'I'm not certain I know where Armani is.'

'Take a taxi, pet.' He took a twenty-pound note from his wallet and handed it to her. 'And you better head home, Duncan – just as soon as you've drafted that email. You'll put a full tank of petrol into our new staff BMW. Go for a rest in a darkened room for a while. I want you to be fully fit for tonight.'

'Why?' Sinclair said. 'What's happening tonight?'

'You and I,' Maclean said, 'are taking off on a long journey.'

16

At quarter past six MacAskill drove the Caravelle off the Kingston Bridge and onto St Vincent Street where he parked and locked the vehicle within walking distance from Casa Alberto. He entered the bar section beyond the dining area and sat at a table in the corner near the back, keeping his eyes fixed on the doorway. After ordering a bottle of beer from the waitress he took out a pen and a sheet of paper and began to write. At the same time as the girl brought his beer to the table Campbell strode into the bar wearing a cream-coloured cotton blazer with a pink shirt, button-down collar, and yellow silk tie. He stopped abruptly in front of MacAskill and stared down at him.

'You asked me to meet you here, Calum Iain,' Campbell said. 'What's bothering you?'

'Oh, I wouldn't say "bothering" me,' MacAskill said. 'It's just, what it is, you know . . . I'm a wee bit concerned about something I heard last night.'

'What's that?'

'I met Kate Morrison last night,' MacAskill said, 'in the cocktail bar of the Nevis after the gig.'

'And?'

'You know the girl from Scalpay who works for *Rèidio na Gaidhealtachd*?'

'Intimately,' Campbell said. 'Get on with it.'

'She was saying,' MacAskill said, 'while we were talking back and forth, you know, one or two things that kind of surprised me.'

'Uh-huh,' Campbell said.

'She told me the Camus Centre was packed last night,' MacAskill said.

'Are you trying to tell me, Calum Iain, that you weren't there yourself last night?' Campbell said. 'Or were you so into the reels and jigs you were rattling out on stage you thought you were elsewhere? As you well know, the Camus Centre was "louping" last night. We all put on a "chanking" show, called, incidentally, the Don Campbell Show. What about it, Calum Iain? Spit it out.'

'Well, she was talking about the money we took in,' MacAskill said. 'She knew all the figures.'

'Uh-huh,' Campbell said.

MacAskill withdrew a sheet of paper from the inside pocket of his jacket and placed it carefully on the table between himself and Campbell.

'You can forget about that piece of paper,' Campbell said. 'Any figures you want to find out about, talk to me.'

'Well,' MacAskill said, 'I was just, you know, like, wondering . . .'

'If there was a bit more in it for you,' Campbell said. 'Isn't that what you've been trying to say?'

'Not really,' MacAskill said. 'That wasn't the main thing. I wanted to ask you if you were thinking of doing any more nights like that. That's all.'

'You're lying, Calum Iain,' Campbell said, 'but I'm

going to tell you the unadulterated truth. Last night, that was a good night. But I'm afraid I won't be doing any more nights like it.'

'Why not?' MacAskill said. 'We made a lot of money.'

'What did you say, Calum Iain?' Campbell said. ' "We made a lot of money", is that it? Sober up, man. It wasn't "we" who made a lot of money. It was me who made a lot of money. How many people would turn out on a cold, rainy night to listen to you, do you think? Or to Mary for that matter? You know I love that girl with all my heart, but I'm afraid she couldn't fill a portacabin on her own. You know, Calum Iain, that what I'm saying is undeniable.'

'That's your opinion,' MacAskill said. 'Still, I reckon you took advantage of Mary and me last night.'

'Do you want to know how much I made?' Campbell said.

'I certainly do,' MacAskill said. 'I'd love to find out how much more than us you got.'

'Okay,' Campbell said. 'Television work first: seven hundred and fifty from Albion. Out of that I paid expenses for your van, petrol, food, wages for you and Mary – and the local dancers – and three separate hotel rooms. That left me with less than nine hundred pounds. But I owe them five hundred. That means I was lucky to get four hundred for myself.'

'What happened to the money from the door?' MacAskill said.

'Don't know if it's any of your business,' Campbell said. 'I'll explain briefly, Calum Iain. After the Camus Centre got their whack, I was left with a third of the net profit. I'm not telling you what that came to because it has nothing to do with you. Carol Macleod took my trousers down – two thirds to Albion and only a third to me! – however, I accepted her terms. What else could I do? Foolishly, I thought I'd get over it. But I didn't, Calum Iain. I was smiling when I got weighed in last night, but I wasn't happy. Nor am I today. There's no doubt about it: I took a screwing from the Albion people last night. Probably when it came to my turn I was a wee bit hard on you guys. Without a shadow of a doubt, despite everything, I made out quite well last night, and you didn't do too badly either.'

'But what I got out of it was a crumb compared to how you made out,' MacAskill said.

'Come here, Calum Iain,' Campbell said, 'so I can give you a piece of advice. As you know, I don't get any pleasure from the gigs nowadays. I had no desire to do that concert last night. I did it. Under a lousy contract. But having accepted the deal I didn't moan or complain about anything. I got the impression however that you were mad to do the concert. You did it, and I did my best to get the best possible money I could. Now you're complaining. You'll really have to stop comparing yourself with other people.'

'Still,' MacAskill said, 'I don't think you divided the money fairly.'

'Calum Iain,' Campbell said, 'you're not listening. There will always be relative deprivation. It's an evil thing, but there are no support agencies. You've got to get over it by yourself. Och, what's the use of talking? I'm not even listening myself to what I'm saying.' He took his wallet out of the hip pocket of his trousers and extracted three banknotes, sixty pounds in total.

'Put that away, Donald,' MacAskill said. 'Knock that on the head, right now.'

'I've got the rap down,' Campbell said, 'but I'm not listening to my own lyrics.' He counted out another two notes and placed them on the table. 'See and buy a nice present for Mary.'

MacAskill slowly picked up the banknotes and stared at them for a good while. He got to his feet, extended his right hand to Campbell, then abruptly withdrew it. He gave a heavy sigh and said, 'Donald, tell me truthfully – what did you make out of it last night?'

Campbell offered his own right hand, which was not accepted. He shrugged. 'Calum Iain,' he said, 'I got a bit of freedom from daft wee troubles for a short time. Oh, these troubles'll come back, but today I'm free, and it's a marvellous feeling.'

'It's good that someone's feeling marvellous,' MacAskill said. 'I'll be seeing you, Mr Campbell.' And he left the bar, moving quickly.

Campbell ordered a bottle of Sol from the waitress. 'Put it on my tab, too, please.' The girl glided off. 'Regret, Donald, lad,' he mumbled to himself, 'you're going to regret all this some day.'

17

Sinclair joined the A822 at Greenloaning and drove north-ward to Crieff. 'Lovely countryside round here,' Maclean said as the BMW passed birch trees on either side of the road. 'The farmers have good land hereabouts. And their farms cover quite a lot of it, too. You'd have to have a fair bit of money before you could afford to buy a place in Perthshire. Anderson at North Television must have a stack of dough to afford a place out here. That's how I'm going to finish up as well. Something classy in this part of the world. A beautiful spot indeed.'

'It certainly is,' Sinclair said, 'but would you fancy staying so far out of town?'

'Well, I don't see many pubs out this way right enough,' Maclean said. 'But I could surely order drink in. That is, if I had a drouth – I'm as dry as a cork this very minute. What time is it?'

'You don't need a drink just now, John Alex,' Sinclair said. 'It's only eight o'clock. We'll be at Anderson's place in quarter of an hour. How long do you think the meeting will last? Maybe half an hour? We'll take off around nine and we'll be back in Glasgow by half past ten. It's a certainty, you'll manage a pint in the Ben easily. What do you think?'

Maclean shook his head in disagreement. 'No, that's too

141

long to wait,' he said. 'Stop at the next hotel you see – there's one in Braco, if my memory serves me right – and get me a half-bottle.' He handed over a ten-pound note to his driver.

'I pity you, John Alex,' Sinclair said. 'You must have a fair skinful in you just now. We passed Braco, umh, about five minutes ago, man. We'll be arriving inside ten minutes. Can you not hold your horses until we get this daft meeting over with? I don't know why we're coming all this way to see the man anyway.'

'You'll soon find out,' Maclean said. 'Did you send that email we discussed earlier?'

'I didn't personally,' Sinclair said. 'I wrote the letter as you asked me to, and I gave it to Donna before I left for home.'

'Oh well,' Maclean said, 'he'll have got it definitely, then. She's a pretty capable girl that Donna, you know. Pretty well put-together, too.' He stretched out in the passenger sear and placed his hands behind his neck. 'You know, Duncan,' he said, 'you should try and treat her in a nicer manner. Is there something about her that puts you off her?'

'What's not to like about the lovely Donna?' Sinclair said. 'The danger is you could get to like her too much. I'd be very willing to make a fool of myself with her, if I ever got the chance. Don't know how the wife would take it, though. I find it hard enough to keep one woman satisfied, never mind trying to keep two of them happy. The bride would sentence me to death by stoning if I as much as looked at another woman.'

142

'Your attitude is so fifties, Duncan,' Maclean said. 'That's the way your parents thought. Life today means that almost all the people I know – men and women – think nothing of separating, getting divorced and taking up with new partners. How many married couples do you know in our business who are happily married? Or how many people in television are married at all?'

'Me and Anne Marie,' Sinclair said.

'Give us a break,' Maclean said. What I'm referring to are "big" people. People like me, for example – separated. Anderson, the man we're going to call on tonight – separated. Angus John at the STG – separated. Campbell himself – separated. That young man – what do you call him? – Ciarán MacRitchie, think he's buckled anyway. Old Flora, the Benbecula woman – well, it's no wonder her man went up the touchline on her. Looking at that face too long would make any man scarper. May God forgive me for mocking his work, but it can't be helped – she is ugly. She was a schoolteacher before she got the job with the STG. The kind of teacher who motivated her charges with extreme vigour. She motivated the children of Castlemilk so vigorously they used to break into the school at night and spray-paint her name with scurrilous comments attached on every wall in the building. I don't know how I retain my sanity when I think about some of the losers I'm obliged to deal with now.' He breathed deeply.

'And that's not even mentioning George Kerr,' he said, 'and I'd forgotten about the Albion people. They're nothing but a tribe of tinkers. As I was telling you, if you conducted a poll among the media folk, with the

143

exception of George Kerr and lower-echelon people like yourself, Duncan, hardly anybody has remained married. I'm telling you, my man, this television lark's hard work. It ruins many a marriage.' He rubbed the inside of the windscreen with the back of his hand.

'Now, Duncan,' he said, 'make a left here. Carry on for about a hundred yards until you come to a T-junction. Turn left, continue for half a mile until you see a big house, all in white, at the top of a rise on your right-hand side. That's Strathearn Lodge, the home of Anderson.'

Sinclair guided the BMW carefully up a fairly steep driveway until he reached a covered entrance flanked by two white columns. They both got out and picked their way up a series of marble steps. Maclean tugged at the old-fashioned door-pull. The door swung open. Before them George Kerr stood in a striped shirt with the sleeves rolled up.

'What on earth?' Maclean said.

Kerr smiled and invited them in with a wave of his arm. He did not say a word.

Maclean said, 'What are you doing here? Where's Anderson?'

'This way, please,' Kerr said.

In an oak-panelled library surrounded by hundreds of books and half a dozen oil paintings of Highland lochs and bens, Anderson sat in a leather chair behind a highly polished cherrywood table. His hands were folded in his lap. He looked at his watch. 'I'll make this brief,' he said. 'We're letting you go, John Alex. For six weeks now George here has been furnishing me with detailed accounts of defalcation, immorality and general incompetence on your part. After due deliberation, the Board of North Television has decided to withdraw all financial support from Iomhaigh Productions. I have informed Angus John Mackenzie at the STG of our decision, and instructed him to cancel your current commission – this *Take a Chance* thing you're supposed to be doing shortly – and I have instructed our agents to initiate legal action against you personally with the purpose of reclaiming the start-up money we advanced to you when your company took out articles.' He glanced at his watch. 'Anything else?' he said to Kerr.

'His signature on the press release, Gordon,' Kerr said. 'That'll clean things up. I haven't abandoned the idea of broadcasting this series, you know. I'll give MacKenzie at the STG a kick up the backside tomorrow and see if they can dig up another independent production company.'

'You bastard,' Maclean said. 'You vile bastard!'

'George, you mean?' Anderson said. 'That's no way to talk to the largest shareholder in North Television, John Alex. You should have been more discreet in your lobbying, vigorous though it was.'

'Didn't you receive my email?' Maclean said.

'No email was received at North from Iomhaigh Productions,' Anderson said.

'But,' Maclean said, 'the email was supposed . . . it would have explained to you, Gordon, my, ah, artistic misgivings, my doubts about the Philistine George Kerr. Are you sure you didn't receive it?'

'John Alex,' Kerr said, 'I don't give a flying fig about

your so-called misgivings. That little Donna was probably too busy on the telephone this afternoon discussing whips and chains with the boyfriend to get near the computer. Not that she would have been able to operate it anyway.

'In any case, what good would it have done you, even if Gordon here had received your pathetic little fiction? I had already decided to flay the skin off your back long before today.'

'You,' Maclean said, 'you would have gone over the head of . . . he had prejudged the situation, Gordon. He's only executive producer for *Cuid do Chroinn*. You're the CEO of North Television. He's overriding your position.'

'That's right,' Anderson said.

'What?'

'Look, Doctor Maclean,' Anderson said, 'George is a member of the board of North and has, over the years, through prudence and foresight, acquired more voting shares in the company than anyone else. This leaves him – and I'm probably guilty of understatement here – this has left George Kerr in an extremely powerful position indeed. If, or rather when, some large broadcaster makes a run at us – Albion maybe or the Liverpool mob, or some massive conglomerate from continental Europe, who knows? – if somebody makes a hostile bid, then George has us all, me included, by the . . . er, well, over a barrel. If he decides to sell out, at a particular price, then he becomes a millionaire and the rest of us are out of work. If he holds on, then he and every other executive gets to come to work for a while longer.

'From a consideration of all this, it should be clear to

you, John Alex, that when George Kerr wants the board to take a particular course of action, we tend to, ah, we *always* accommodate him. Your views, whether expressed orally or in writing are simply not germane.'

Maclean did not take his eyes of Kerr. 'Oh, no,' he said, 'oh no. Angus John and the rest of the STG will never approve of this.'

'John Alex,' Kerr said, 'you still don't understand, do you? What are you thinking of: "Angus John will never approve this"? We made Angus John, just as we made you.' He turned towards Anderson. 'Didn't make too good a job of them, eh, Gordon? One of them a fat wet-head and the other a *cockroach*.'

'Could we move on, George, please,' Anderson said. 'I've a meeting with the Disney people in Burbank tomorrow, and I'll have to be sharp discussing US adaptations of a couple of our most acclaimed shows. I dread meeting that Chinese-Jewish accountant they've got over there again.' He passed a sheet of paper over to Maclean. 'Sign this, please, John Alex. Usual guff about "artistic differences" and "Dr Maclean seeking challenges in other areas of artistic endeavour".' He handed him a fountain pen.

Maclean did not read the press release. His gaze did not waver from Kerr. 'What if I refuse to sign?'

'You know something?' Kerr said. 'You are an arsehole, all right? What's more, John Alex, you're a double-barrelled arsehole. I don't understand it. Every single one of you guys who have the double-barrelled Christian name, you're all on the mentally disabled list. Must be a sign

147

from above. "Lady somewhere on the planet has given birth to a donkey? Give it a double-barrelled name." You people, all you Donald Johns and John Anguses and Mary Margarets and Flora Theresas, all of you *Teuchters*, doesn't matter how hard we try to make you see sense and tell you what's best for you: "Do it our way. We've been in television a long time, right? We know the business." You're all the same way, and you've got the same attitude, too, John Alex. You're like all those retards saying, "Let's have the service based in the communities at community-hall level." Listen, how embarrassing is that? Get it into your heads,' he said to Sinclair, 'when it comes to making programmes, we, the English-speaking majority, have the expertise. You *peasants* with your poxy seventeen million – to provide programming for less than one per cent of the Scottish population, mind you – have come late to the table. The big boys were here first. And if you want a game, we'll take your money. But you'll play by our rules.'

'I'm not signing,' Maclean said.

'Suit yourself, Dr Maclean,' Anderson said. 'The release is going out tomorrow.'

Kerr gave a deep sigh. 'It never fails. Try to be nice to those bastards, get some kind of defiance. Must be the acid rain up in the islands or something. Watch my lips, Maclean. You. Are. Finished. Now just get in the breeze. Now.'

'Come on, John Alex,' Sinclair said, and he turned abruptly and walked out of the library.

Maclean stood motionless for about half a minute before

he too made his departure from Strathearn Lodge. As he arrived at the canopied front entrance he saw the BMW moving slowly down the gravel driveway towards the main road.

An owl in the trees behind the grand dwelling hooted plaintively.

18

At half past nine on Friday morning at the outer doors of the office of Iomhaigh Productions, Duncan Sinclair made yet another attempt to turn the key in the lock. Once again he failed. Sweat poured from every pore, and a violent tremor assailed his entire body. He had put the key back in his pocket and retreated a couple of steps from the door when he heard the hinges squeaking. Tears were in his eyes when he saw Donna MacIver, dressed in a short leather skirt and cropped top, standing in the doorway, a broad grin on her face and with her arms spread wide in welcome. Without uttering a word Sinclair moved towards her, placed his arms round about her and rested his cheek on the smooth, warm skin of her shoulder. 'Donna,' he said faintly, 'I'm sorry.'

'Shush, you big fool,' Donna said, gently rubbing the back of his head with her hand. 'Nothing bad's going to happen to you. Come on in along with me.' She took him by the hand and pulled him into the office, keeping up a flow of conversation all the time. 'They changed the locks yesterday. That's why you had trouble trying to get in. She pushed open the door leading to the smaller office and raised her voice: 'Guess who I found behind the door? There you go, Duncan, away you go in and I'll make you a cup of coffee.' Swiftly she took his face in both hands and kissed him open-mouthed. She leaned back, made fluttering movements with her tongue and departed for the kitchen.

Sinclair closed his eyes for a few seconds, inhaled noisily and walked into the room. Seated at a chair next to the only window in the little room was Ciarán MacRitchie, drinking a cup of coffee. Sinclair moved briskly towards his desk and quickly opened the bottom drawer. 'Excuse me,' he said, 'I used to work here.'

'Whatever are you trying to say, darling?' MacRitchie said. 'What's wrong with you?'

'Sorry about this,' Sinclair said as he wrenched the top off a quarter bottle of whisky and swallowed swiftly a mouthful of its contents. 'I'm Duncan Sinclair.' He coughed violently. 'Sorry, who're you?'

'Oh, I know who you are alright,' MacRitchie said, and he walked over to the desk and stretched out his right hand. 'Ciarán MacRitchie, the new head of Iomhaigh Two.' He took the bottle from Sinclair and took a small sip out of it. 'Where have you been, man? Everybody's been worried sick about you and looking for you everywhere.'

'Who,' Sinclair said, 'has been looking for me?'

'Me,' Macritchie said, 'young Donna, Angus John, Anderson. Lots of people were missing you, Duncan.'

'Where's Maclean?' Sinclair said.

'For all we care,' said MacRitchie, 'he could be in St Kilda.'

'And Kerr,' Sinclair said, 'where's he?'

'Oh, he'll still be singing your praises,' MacRitchie said,

152

'to anyone who'll listen to him, I expect. He thinks you're a very able lad, Duncan. I was talking to him at a meeting in Stornoway yesterday, and he filled me in on everything that happened in Crieff last Tuesday night. And his advice to me was, if I found you, I was to keep a tight grip of you.'

'You're joking, aren't you?' Sinclair said.

'No, straight up, dear,' MacRitchie said. 'Believe me, I'm not joking. We're going to need a guy like you big time, and I have the authority to give you a salary increase.' He slid a paper on to the desk in front of Sinclair. 'It's a new contract. Have a look at it, and sign it when you've got a minute. I'm pretty sure you'll find it appealing.' He made his way back to the chair by the window and raised his coffee cup. 'Where on earth have you been for the past two days anyway?'

'I've been behind the moon,' Sinclair said. 'I don't have any recollection of leaving Anderson's house that night. All I can remember is that I stopped at a branch of Victoria Wine in Perth. I bought a couple of litre-bottles of whisky there and booked into the Salutation Hotel. I was between the bed and the toilet for a full day and two nights. Yesterday morning I managed with difficulty to get out for more drink, and that was me, a sodden heap in the bed all last night. In the middle of the night sometime – it was still dark anyway – I phoned Anne Marie and she told me, that unless I brought me and the car back to Glasgow today, she was going to take off with the wee one to Eriskay tomorrow. I haven't touched a drop today – well, until just now – and that's what leaving me so shaky, withdrawal from booze.'

'We'll soon have you dried out, darling,' MacRitchie said. 'Me and Donna.'

'Good to hear it,' Sinclair said.

'Oh, you've nothing to worry about with the new team that's supporting you now,' MacRitchie said.

'You'll have to forgive me,' Sinclair said. 'I'm all turned about today. I don't know what you're talking about.'

'It's simple,' MacRitchie said. 'I'm the new leader-off here at Iomhaigh Two. I never really fancied Stornoway that much at all. That place would put the stones to sleep. But since Kerr still seems to be quite keen to carry on with *Cuid do Chroinn* with Campbell as the presenter, and since we couldn't find another independent production company in the time available – don't we have to start filming next Wednesday? – as I was saying, because the deadline was approaching so quickly, Anderson came up with the idea that all we had to do was change the name of this company. And, naturally, appoint a new CEO down here. They asked me to take on the responsibility. And that's all, she said. Shake on it, pal.'

'Does that mean,' Sinclair said, 'that I don't have to empty my desk? I've still got work to do here?'

'You'll have too much work to do,' MacRitchie said. 'You're the only person in here who knows how to make programmes. Donna and I have only to try and help you get everything ready for Wednesday. Now, tell us about Campbell. Do you think he's ready and raring to go?'

'There was a wee kind of *thing* happening,' Sinclair said, 'some kind of obstacle in the way, something to do

154

with outstanding money Campbell owed. Some debt was worrying him, or so I heard.'

'I know all about that,' MacRitchie said. 'STG or North, I can't remember which one, they're going . . . um . . . they made a decision yesterday to forget all about that little financial matter.'

'Campbell will be delighted at that outcome,' Sinclair said, 'when he hears about it.'

'And well he might be,' MacRitchie said. 'Will you let him know that we want him in here first thing on Monday morning? He's got two days' rehearsal. He'll get paid two hundred pounds a day, meals and drinks included. And tell him he'll get the fee you promised him for each programme just as soon as we start putting footage in the can on Wednesday.'

'Right you are,' Sinclair said. 'I'll give him a bell straight away. Will his sister Peggy know where he is?'

Before he could lift the receiver Donna MacIver entered holding a steaming mug in her hands. 'There you go, darling,' she said, going down on one knee revealing a generous expanse of shapely thigh. 'Take this with my undying love. Drink it quickly, now. I've put a dash of something in it. Take it nice and slow. Don't want you choking.' She maintained her position, gazing at Sinclair as he drank.

After swallowing about half the contents of the mug, Sinclair grunted with satisfaction and smiled. 'Marvellous. This is just marvellous. I think I'm already feeling better.' He took another sip from the mug. 'Fair Michael of the Golden Reins,' he said, as he struggled to rise from the chair, with Donna MacIver trying to restrain him by wrapping her arms around his waist and letting her full breasts fall onto his lap. 'I forgot about Anne Marie,' he said. 'I better phone her. I've got to tell her I've still got a job. She'll hardly believe it.' He looked at MacRitchie. 'May I phone, Ciarán?'

'You can do whatever you like, Duncan' MacRitchie said. 'Hey, it's true that I'm the gaffer. In name, that is. But you're the gaffer in reality in this place, know what I mean?'

On her knees by now with her upper body pressed tight against Sinclair's chest, Donna MacIver made herself comfortable by scattering two or three little cushions around her hips and raised her eyes to Sinclair's face. 'Duncan, love,' she said, 'let me phone your wife.' She moistened her carmine-red lips with her tongue. 'I'll tell her you're safe and that I myself am taking care of you.'

'Donna, my treasure,' Sinclair said, with a rueful smile on his lips, 'in my eyes, pet, you are my moon and my sun. To me, my treasure, you are my guide and my star.'

'Oh, Duncan,' Donna said, 'thank you. That's so beautiful.'

'That's to me,' Sinclair said. 'To Anne Marie, my wife, I don't know. You'd be – how to put it delicately? – in the eyes of my wife you'd be something different. I'll phone her myself. Let's not put a bad complexion on a day that's started out so promising up till now.'

156

19

Calum Iain MacAskill's feet stuttered to a halt in front of number four Park Terrace. He peered closely at the names engraved on the brass plates on the wall. When he saw the letters ITR, he put his finger on the button beside them. He heard a crackling sound and a woman's voice came out of the metal screen where his hand rested.

'Hello?' the voice said.

'Hello,' MacAskill said.

'State your business.'

MacAskill bent down and placed his lips close to the grille. 'I'd like to make a complaint,' he said. 'I'm here to see . . . to make a complaint about, to register a complaint with regard to . . . er, low wages in television.'

'What's the name?'

'I don't know,' MacAskill said. 'Anybody would do.'

'Sir,' the voice said sharply, 'what is *your* name?'

'Malcolm John MacAskill.'

'Look, Mr MacAskill,' the voice said, 'it's half past four on a Friday. Why don't you come back on Monday morning?'

'No,' MacAskill said. 'You listen to me. I'm going home to Harris tomorrow and I can't make it on Monday. Or any other day.' He became very angry and began to shout. 'It'll be a cold day in hell before I ever come back to this toilet of a town.'

'Sir,' the voice said in an angry tone, 'get away from that door this very minute. If you don't clear off, I'm sending for security.'

MacAskill lost it completely. He was extremely uncomfortable anyway crouched down at first whispering, now bellowing, into a metal grille in broad daylight. 'That's great,' he shouted. 'That's really great. Security'll back up my story. The one I'm going to the newspapers with.' From the corner of his eye he saw something or someone moving on the pavement below. A young girl, about nine years of age, was bent double laughing loudly as she observed his antics above her on the steps. MacAskill turned his back on her to block out her irritating presence. 'Look, lady, I've told you who I am – Malcolm John MacAskill, Seventeen Nua Ard, Isle of Harris. I have official business with the Independent Television Registry. I am making a legitimate complaint against the franchise holders for southern Scotland. I have a very real grievance against Albion Television. You know how much they paid me last Friday? For *three* television programmes I recorded for them in Fort William? Never mind. The press boys'll be interested. And I'm going to tell them that the ITR wouldn't even let me past the door.' He slapped the screen with some force and spat on the steps. He turned to leave. As he did so, a screech came from the sound box. He bent down and put his ear close to the perforations in the grille.

'Mr MacAskill?' a voice said, a man's voice this time.

'Yes?'

'Mr Traynor will see you,' the voice said. 'Wait one moment, please.'

A faint click sounded from the lock. MacAskill looked up to the heavens that were now slowly darkening, stood upright and took a deep breath. 'About time, you useless lot,' he whispered softly. With one finger he pushed open the outside door of the ITR and walked inside.

20

As Donald Campbell, on foot, turned into Govan Road at half past five on Wednesday evening after visiting the bank, he immediately noticed a brand new Land-Rover Discovery parked at the close where Gretta lived. He climbed the stairs and he was on the point of inserting the key into the lock when the door opened.

Gretta stood in the doorway with a warning finger held to her lips to intimate that she had a visitor. She was dressed in jeans and a sleeveless white cotton top. She wore neither shoes nor stockings and the glow on her skin revealed that she had newly come out of the shower. 'What kept you, Donald?' she whispered. 'That man's been waiting for you for half an hour at least.'

'Who is it?'

'Mr Miller from Albion TV.'

'I'll not take too long,' Campbell said, 'getting rid of him. Get dressed and doll yourself up. We're going out tonight.'

'Oh, you're so commanding, Donald,' Gretta said. 'Your kind invitation kindly accepted.' She went into the bedroom.

Campbell entered the kitchen where Gus Miller sat in an overstuffed chair covered in dark green tartan fabric. Miller was resplendent in hip-length mountaineering jacket, a faded tartan shirt, jeans and cowboy boots. He was enjoying the warmth from a roaring fire and also the coffee he was drinking with relish from a tall mug.

'Gus, my man,' Campbell said, 'how's it going? Is that your Discovery out there?'

'It is,' Miller said. 'I'm off to Aonach Mor for some skiing after this. They're good in the snow. What are you driving yourself these days?'

'I don't have a car at all,' Campbell said. 'Not that you need one in the city. I've got to admit I keep looking at the adverts in the papers, though.

'Well, maybe I'll be able to help you in that respect,' Miller said. 'Do you remember the contract you signed for me a while back?'

'That thing about Venezuela?' Campbell said. 'Yeah, I remember it vividly. Thank you for the fee.'

'Do you like doing that kind of work?'

'Listen, Gus,' Campbell said, 'I like any kind of work. Just as long as I get paid for it.'

'I really do think,' Miller said, 'it's about time we put this relationship we have on a more . . . um, *formal* basis, know what I mean?'

'Not really,' Campbell said. 'What do you mean?'

'Well, you know that research you did on that rogue MacGregor? We need more ideas like that. And we'll pay you for them. What I'd like is for you to come into us with your proposals for television programmes, and we'll put you on a one-year contract. How does that grab you?'

'One year?' Campbell said.

'Uh-huh.'

'How many ideas would you want in that time?' Campbell said.

'As many as you can come up with,' Miller said. 'You won't be the only person doing this kind of work for us, you know.'

'I won't?' Campbell said. 'Who else have you got working for you?'

'Pshaw! We've got a whole heap of folk out there working for us. Some of them are pretty prolific. Others aren't.'

'Would I know any of them?' Campbell said.

'I'm pretty sure you would,' Miller said. 'The majority of them are journalists or lecturers in the colleges and universities, and they mostly deal in English programming. But I'd want you, Donald, to be involved in coming up with ideas for Gaelic programmes.'

'And how hard would the work be?'

'Don't worry about that just now, Donald,' Miller said. 'Professor Calderwood whom we have on a retainer calls his monthly cheque "hingin' aboot money". Hey, it's not a fortune, but with expenses, it'll give you a nice piece of change at the end of the month.'

'What are you offering?'

'I'm prepared to give you,' Miller said, 'twenty-five thousand pounds a year as well as any reasonable expenses you incur performing your duties – travel, books, periodicals, membership of libraries, stuff like that. It'd come to a little under two grand net a month. You'd send everything you wrote once every four weeks or so, I'll have a look at it and we'll arrange to meet for a working lunch somewhere.'

'Just as long as it's not in the Poorhouse,' Campbell said. 'I've really bad memories of Chez Maurice.'

'No, we'll body-swerve old Maurice,' Miller said laughingly. 'Oh, I almost forgot – Carol sends her love. She's totally in love with the stuff they shot in Fort William. And she wants to give you two thousand as a fee. What she said was: "Tell Donald he's a very funny man, though he can't tell the difference between a third and a half." She said you'd understand that.'

Gretta came into the room wearing a green silk kimono that left her midriff bare and contoured her shapely breasts. 'What'll you have to drink, Mr Miller?' she said. 'I think we've got some wine in. Would you like a glass of Chilean red?'

'No, I won't have anything, thanks,' Miller said. 'I'm just going now. I'll give you peace to have your food.'

'Oh, we're eating out tonight,' Gretta said, 'but I think I'll have a wee glass of wine before we go.' She gave Campbell her attention. 'What'll you have, Donald? Cappuccino? Coke?' He said he would prefer coffee and both men watched her as she prepared the drinks.

Eventually, Miller broke the silence. 'You're a very lucky man, Donald.' He leaned forward and lowered his voice. 'What's the relationship between the pair of you?'

'I call Gretta my daughter,' Campbell said.

'She looks like you.'

'She's not really mine,' Campbell said. 'But that's what I call her: "my daughter". To be truthful, she's my daughter, my sister, my mate. I don't really understand

164

the bond between us: Gretta's the brightest ray of sun-shine in my entire life just now.'

Gretta came over to where Campbell was sitting and handed him a cup of cappuccino. 'There you go, old man,' she said and took a sip from her glass of Merlot, leaving crimson lipstick streaks on the rim. 'Hold your tongue, and drink your coffee.'

'Well, I'll leave the contract with you,' Miller said. He placed a white envelope on the mantelpiece. 'Have a look at it, and if there's anything in it you find disturbing, you can give me a bell in Edinburgh next week. I'm in the office until Thursday. Okay?'

'I'm going to be fairly busy next week, Gus,' Campbell said. 'I'm starting to film a series of programmes for Iomhaigh Two in the North studio in Perth – when is it again? – next Wednesday. That's not a problem for you, is it?'

'Not at all,' Miller said. 'You're free, Donald, to work for anybody at all. You can carry on with the gigs if you like. Hey, you're a mercenary, that's what you are. All I want are your ideas, do you understand?'

'As far as I can see,' Campbell said, 'there doesn't seem to be any kind of obstacle attached to your proposition. I think we'd better settle this thing right now. Just give me a minute or two until I digest this.' He slit open the envelope and took the contract out.

Gretta asked Miller again if he'd like a glass of wine, and once again he declared he was fine as he was.

'Hey!' Campbell said. 'What's this?'

'What?' Miller said.

'The date,' Campbell said. 'You've dated this contract

Saturday, the twelfth of February. That was five weeks ago, man.'

'That's right,' Miller said. 'That's the day I commissioned you to write the piece on Venezuela.'

'So, the contract started last month?'

'Yes, and that means that we at Albion are a bit late in paying your monthly retainer, doesn't it? He shook his head as though astonished at this oversight and took out his wallet. 'I'll give you what we owe you right this minute. It'll be cash, I'm afraid. If you write a wee note saying you've received your monthly payment, I'll be grateful.'

'You're in a terrible hurry to get my name on a contract,' Campbell said. 'Why's that?'

'I'm experiencing a high level of shame,' Miller said. 'OK, I'll come clean with you. I must have written evidence that you were on our books as an adviser before we recorded that concert you did for us in Fort William.'

'Why?'

'Because the ITR are all over me like a cheap suit,' Miller said. 'They've received a complaint from someone about inadequate compensation for a gig this person allegedly took part in. They're demanding that I show them copies of the contracts we offered the cast of the show. I am unwilling to do this. Mainly because they don't exist. But I can't admit this.'

'How do you think you're going to get away with this?'

' "Staff" is the answer,' Miller said. 'If the producer of the programme was a member of our staff – that's you, Donald – what business is it of theirs what kind of fees we pay artists? If you put your name to that contract you have in your hand, Donald, I can then go to the ITR and the STG as well and say to them all: "Get out of my face, you lot!" And that's what I'd like to do.'

'That's what you'd like to do, is it?' Campbell said.

'That's what I must do. You have got to be connected to Albion Television, Donald. Not from today. But starting in February.'

Campbell lifted up the contract and smiled. 'As the Good Book says, "Whatsoever a man sows, that shall he also reap." ' He stretched his free hand out. 'Can I get a loan of your pen, Gus?'

Miller handed over a fountain pen with a gold nib, and Campbell signed the contract. Miller got to his feet and lifted the contract from the table. As he busied himself with the numerous zips of his outer jacket he said, 'Sincere thanks and deep abasements from me for being so obliging, Donald. And thank you, Gretta, for – um, many thanks to you both for your hospitality and for being so . . . so . . . *wholesome*. You needn't be in any hurry, Donald, about sending material over to us.'

'Don't worry, Gus,' Campbell said, 'I won't be. Party time, I think.' He shook Miller's hand warmly and escorted him to the door. When he returned to the kitchen there was no sign of Gretta. He entered the bedroom where he found her lying on the bed looking up at him with glittering eyes. He stood at the top of the bed and began to take bundles of banknotes out of his pockets and shower them on top of her. By the time he had emptied his pockets the young blonde was giggling helplessly beneath a carpet of cash.

167

'Gretta, light of my life,' Campbell said, 'I want you to do the rounds of the estate agents tomorrow and see if you can get a rented flat for yourself, out of this tip. Hillhead or Hyndland would be nice. Get away from that piece of trash downstairs. I won't be living with you, pet. Well, let's see what happens – maybe I'll spend the odd night in yours now and again – but I'm going to get a small place for myself.'

'Why do you want us to live apart?'

Campbell did not answer.

'Do you want the freedom to sleep with other girls?'

'Leave it out, Gretta!' Campbell said. 'I'm not answering that.'

'Whoa, is that a yes?' Gretta said. 'You're a man, Donald, you have needs. I don't expect you to live like a monk.'

'It's none of your business how I choose to live.'

'Don't you love me?' Gretta said.

'That's quite enough.'

'Let me love you, then,' Gretta said.

'No, you can't do that, Gretta.'

'OK, I'm able to give you a wee bit of time. Can I ask you one question?'

'Sure.'

'Do you think you might love me?'

Campbell smiled. 'Sure, that's almost a definite.'

'Good enough for me.' And she raised both arms in a gesture of welcome. 'You know, old man, you're welcome to come to me any time. I'd be good to you. You must know that.'

'I know,' Campbell said, 'but I've never liked to be tied to one place for very long. It's immature, I know, but I like to be on the move.'

'What is it you're looking for, Donald?'

'All my life,' Campbell said, 'I don't know, I've been trying to reach a particular place. But although I've expended a lot of energy, I never seem to get close to my destination.'

'And where is this destination?'

'Oh, I know where it is all right,' Campbell said. 'But the problem is, dear, I can't get near it, because I don't know where to start. I don't know if you can understand this – at times I don't understand it myself – but before you go on a journey you've got to know where you are, you know, before you take off. Always, ever since leaving the school, I've been like a stag in the mist. But thank the Lord, and yourself, Gretta, I've a better idea of where I am now.'

'You're in 1413 Govan Road.'

'Not for long, though,' Campbell said. 'When you're out shopping tomorrow see if you can pick up a light summer-weight suit for me. Try Fraser's – they've a good gents' department there – or John Lewis. Will you do that for me, love?'

'You're not thinking of going off on a trip, are you, Donald?' Gretta said.

'Maybe.'

'Where?'

'Don't know yet.'

'Are you going alone?'

169

'Well, it was nearly a wasted journey the last trip I took by myself,' Campbell said.

'Are you taking me with you?'

'No,' Campbell said. 'As you know, I'd do anything for you. I'll certainly play the pipes at your wedding. But you've to find a slack-jawed young fellow who'll marry you first. You'll not be able to do that with a white haired old man by your side.' He walked over to the door. 'Get ready, my darling. We've got a splendid big night ahead of us, and tomorrow's not promised to any of us.'

'Donald,' Gretta said, 'where will you go?'

'As they say in Uist,' Campbell said, 'I may go "down north" – to Inverness, know what I mean? – or maybe I'll go "up south" towards the sun. I'm sure there'll be plenty of lonely widows wherever I go.'

He ducked to avoid the pillow Gretta threw at him and launched into a ballad in Spanish as he strode out of the room.